LEARNING
as we
GROW

Motherhood rooted in what God says and research proves

Many blessings!
Jenna Young

JENNA YOUNG, MA BCBA
Behavior Therapist & Christian Mama

Dedicated to the sweet boys who call me "Mom"

— **Drake** & **Zachary** —

Contents

Preface

Even before I became a mom, self-care has always been the solemn quiet of Barnes and Noble for me. After having kids, though, it was my important way to do some "professional development" in the new role. I'd go to the psychology section and find book after thrilling book on the science behind the issues or patterns surrounding motherhood.

I'd dive in while sipping my coffee, but would always walk away a little disconnected. The information was spot-on, but the authors always approached the content from a secular perspective. The spiritual side of me was left dry. They would explain fascinating results and discoveries pertaining how I could do this motherhood thing well, but without any inclusion of God, the contents felt like they were missing a crucial component of research to be deemed credible and worthy. The psychologists, researchers, authors, and stories may have informed me how my brain functions and processes my environment and emotions, but they ended the story there. Incomplete.

As a behavior therapist, I studied and trained to be a master observer. My specialty is focused on changing and helping the way people act—particularly children. It starts with identifying what has been happening before, during, and after an unwanted behavior. The root of most behavior is to acquire a need. Our time walking through the occurrences gives me the clues I need to understand what need is motivating them to do what they do and why. Once I know why, I can help that person reach the need in a different, healthier way. I'm in the field of reading people to discover the reasons behind their actions. Once we understand what their reason for a behavior is, I can provide healthy ways to meet that need and eliminate the negative actions that needed change. Most of the time, my "clients" are parents and their kids, but the kids' ages range, which keeps it interesting!

Then I became a mom, and suddenly I was also the parent with a kid in my own office, trying to figure out how to keep a peaceful household and prevent bad habits. My brain and my heart wanted some guidance. Studying the Bible soothed the heart-ache I felt every time I got confused about my kid's needs. The research provided tools for managing the kids but perhaps not nurturing them the Christ-like way I craved. I recognized the union between the two. Christian parenting books and parenting psy-chology books weren't contradicting each other. They just weren't acknowledging each other in the bookstore.

Here's what I noticed:

Within the world of behavior therapy, science is their capital-T Truth. I'd say it's their Bible, but that'd be misleading as scientific results change and evolve over time. But in behavior therapy, science and the scientific method is what they base all of their practice upon.

Now, I absolutely agree that science is an enriching, informative resource. In that way, it is my lowercase-t truth. I enjoy learning and applying this truth to both my life as well as the life of my clients. This truth brings great benefits. However, I do not agree that science is the *only* truth. I believe that God is our ultimate truth, and He shares that truth in the Bible. The Bible is the absolute Truth that supersedes and should be used as a guidepost for scientific truth. I know I am not alone, as I've also met many believers in the field of behavior analysis. Sadly, the content I'm finding does not meet science truth with God's truth. It's almost as if they think mixing the two would be taboo or ruining the purity of either. It's just an unspoken rule of thumb. *It's easier just to keep it separate.*

I would then wander over to the religion section and find some authors that I saw eye-to-eye with. We could probably chat all day about the great things they had to share about motherhood and their love of the Lord. This is where I felt comfort. This is where I felt I belonged. I mean, these were *my people* after all. I'll be honest here, though. After being filled theologically and relationally, I'd again walk away a bit empty sometimes. I saw the void where research and professionalism sometimes lacked in some author's texts. While warm and encouraging, I closed the books with trust issues. Where were the facts to support what they said? I believed the facts were there, but I failed to see them cited and represented.

I appreciated the way they shared their experiences with and about Jesus—no cita-tions needed for your testimony and wisdom! But when it came time to giving me advice on the big decisions of raising kids, my analytical brain wondered if they could give me more than just a gut feeling. If we are instructing another on something they must do, we need more than just personal experience to justify it. Just because it worked for them does not mean we can replicate it and it will work for everyone. My frustration was not with the authors of the books I read—I am not blaming them. The issue I faced was the general lack of Christian nonfiction books on parenting that applied peer-reviewed, scientific research and studies to their perceptions and suggestions.

Ironically, at my local bookstore, the psychology and religion sections actually mirror one another, yet physically were placed on complete opposite sides. At one point, I even sat at a table and gazed back and forth. It was clear. God was calling me to fill in the gap.

This is a book written by someone who a year ago would not consider herself to be an author. I'm a mom, who happens to be behavior therapist, who is learning how to live out what she knows to be true (both biblically and professionally) every day for her two sweet sons. I've placed my profession at the foot of the cross, and God has called me to use it in this way: a book with acknowledgement, encouragement, explanation, and insight about the mom issues that keep you up at night, searching back and forth between Scripture and Google to find answers.

I know you do this, because I do the same thing. I want both. I want what God tells me to be true, but I also want the practicality that research provides. I want to have patience, but I also want to know how to potty-train this child efficiently! I want to give the truth in love, but I also need to know how to discipline when my child is disobedient.

I do not have all the answers. I'd caution you of parenting books that claim to. I just want to stand in that space between psychology and Scripture and start to show you how you can have both. The space is not division or a border between two camps. It's where God's Word prepares us and educates us on psychology, and how psychology can enlighten and support God's Word. My calling is to explain the union of these two for motherhood.

I know how intimidating the Bible can be. It's a lot to take in even when you believe it, even when you understand some of it, and especially when you don't understand it. When it comes to applying the Bible, truly molding to it as we parent, many of us come up short. It's just too tall a task. You can think of stories of biblical people, but honestly, most of them highlighted are not mothers. They are middle-aged men who are called to sojourn and share the gospel. It's understandable why that would be extremely difficult to apply to motherhood! Rest assured though, there are plenty of passages that we can follow that direct us on how to be our best, even if you are in old workout shorts you've been wearing for two days, chasing three kids under five.

Then I look at research, and I kind of laugh because that's not much less intimidating than the Bible! It may not be as primitive or archaic, but it's a lot of numbers, big words, and vague, conditional conclusions. Worse, we don't even have *access* to most research. Endless studies are conducted every month by those smart people with ten capital letters written after their name. They have put together some incredible studies and theories that relate to how we can be the best moms for our kids. But it's buried in libraries with memberships or other sites that cost money, and doesn't read very accessibly for the sleep-deprived. Don't you worry. I paid tuition money to spend many long hours reading research and learning how to read it. And I'm still that self-proclaimed nerd who reads this stuff for fun. Let me do the hard work for you, and I'll break down the highlights as we go.

I promise that I'll bring you research that is peer-reviewed and has gone through rigorous testing to be deemed legit. And when I say "peer-reviewed," I don't mean by a few of the author's friends. In order for a finding to be considered "peer-reviewed," it must be scrutinized by a group of scholars in that field—usually playing devil's advocate—and live to tell the tale. It must pass through the harshest of critics. Getting anyone to agree these days is tough stuff, so when a piece of work passes, it earns a certain level of trust. There is an epidemic of false information in our culture today, and for the purpose of this book, I chose case studies and theories that are credible through peer review.

I'll be using psychology—which etymologically stems from the word *psyche* and actually means both "soul" and "mind." The word itself helps remind me what the goal is. Ultimately, what I'm after is disseminating how we can use our souls and minds best to apply God's Truth to the trenches of motherhood.

Motherhood is truly one of God's sweetest blessings to us, but it's also quite the task to steward. We can't do this alone, so please don't beat yourself up. Take a swig of that coffee and, if you'll let me, I want to help. We all need someone to walk this journey with. Someone to ride the highs and lows by our side. It would be my privilege to be that person for you. And it'll be kind of tough at times.

When we look at what research shows us about motherhood, we could only wish that we could attain it all. The concepts we will review together are the *best-case scenario*. While this is admittingly a tall task, it's never an excuse to stop trying. Our kiddos give us a fresh start every morning. If the sun rises, we have another chance. Every day is an

Motherhood is truly one of God's sweetest blessings to us, but it's also quite the task to steward. We can't do this alone, so please don't beat yourself up.

opportunity to grow. Every day you are able to be the best mom you can be. The standard is high, but let's go for it. Let's see how close we can get! I think we can all agree our kids are absolutely worth it.

The *best mom we can be*—it would be easy to place our ideal, or our vision of what that person is, and claim it as truth. Set *that* as our goal. Maybe you are thinking of another mom you'd desire to be just like? Maybe it's a fictional character even? Our brains tend to insert our own vision of the *perfect mom* into our minds rather than capturing it from what God's Word and research *actually* have to say. Both have a lot to say about motherhood, and I believe it warrants our attention.

We can't do our best until we know what the best is. When we paint our *best-mom-I can-be* picture from God, it's definable. It's something we can describe and act upon. It's something we can measure. There is so much hope in this way of thinking. Dreaming of being the next Carol Brady or Lorelai Gilmore is not attainable. It's a fictional makeup of what motherhood could be in twenty- or forty-minute increments. We have something better—the real thing—even if it's a bit messier. And we have to get moving because we know the time goes by too fast to wait. Yes, the days are long, but the years are short.

Is your coffee getting cold? Help yourself a refill or two because we have so many exciting things to cover. We will talk about the motherhood bits that are large and scary. The ones we have accepted will just always be hard. The parts of motherhood that we've believed will always just be this way, and also the ones that we've learned to just martyr through.

It won't all be hard stuff. When you read about them, I hope you'll laugh as hard as I did at some of the dumb mistakes I've made! That's a part of learning and growing too.

Motherhood is challenging. That's not something I'm here to "solve," nor should that ever be the goal. Instead, we're going to dive into God's Word and research-based guidance to be those crazy moms who genuinely love every stinkin' day with their kids.

CHAPTER ONE

Growing Out of the Mom Box

When I was a kid, I remember planning to happily follow the "normal" path of life. I'd get married, have kids, and live the happily-ever-after American dream. I'd get the house, the job, and maybe even a porch swing. That "normal path" started off well for me. I graduated college and married the man of my dreams. Everything was going in the right direction—phew! My life was fitting the church lady stories, the movies, and the stories of the other women around me. The *normal* path.

I remember taking a walk around the neighborhood with my sister-in-law after dinner one night. The topic of having children came up, and I shared with her my desire to adopt. It was the first time I shared it with anyone aloud besides my hubby, John.

Ironically, John and I talked about adoption just weeks prior to this walk with my sister-in-law. John and I decided together that not only was adoption something we were open to but something we truly felt called to do. I would hold onto this conversation with my sister-in-law for years. It was like God had been eavesdropping. He heard me say it out loud.

What happened after that was a long struggle of infertility. After much avoidance, I finally went to a specialist, who confirmed I had Stage IV endometriosis. My chances of conceiving were quite slim. That year was a doozy, as I went on to have two surgeries, three rounds of intrauterine insemination (IUI), and four rounds of in vitro fertilization (IVF). If you are a fellow infertility mom, that makes sense to you. If that sounds like a foreign language, it basically means I was a hormone guinea pig.

Nothing worked. Not even a little. I actually came out of the whole ordeal even worse than when I started. I had nerve damage in my thigh from all the shots, and the one surgery actually had adverse effects on my endometriosis, making my pain even worse. Surprisingly, I was still optimistic. I remembered claiming out loud what I felt God calling us to. The time was now. God was telling us to adopt.

While still feeling positive, the adoption process was very long and lonely. We went on to wait not one, two, or even three years. We waited four long years for our sweet son Drake to make it into our home. We were actually waiting to adopt from a different country when we saw a photo of Drake. That is when our whole lives changed. Our story shifted from wanting to be parents to wanting to be *his* parents! We fell in love with him! We wanted nothing more than to bring this boy home.

When we talked to our social worker, she said that switching countries was like moving mountains in the adoption world. So, what did we do? We prayed that God would begin to move the mountains! Let me testify: God did just that. He parted the sea, and we ran through to China to bring our adorable son home.

If that isn't miraculous enough, the Lord then allowed me the privilege of experiencing another side of motherhood, probably one most of you have experienced, which is having a biological child. After thirteen years of praying to conceive, I'll admit my prayers kind of fizzled out. I really didn't think that was the Lord's plan for us, so I basically stopped asking. Ha! Never say never!

Saying I was in shock would be an understatement! It will be a moment of awe I will remember for the rest of my life. A moment that confirmed not only to never to put *motherhood* in a box, but also never to put *God* in a box. His plans are always better than ours. Even if the plan involves tears and pain, He always works it out for our good and His glory. Our son Zachary came at the perfect time, and he was the perfect baby boy. Our boys would be almost 5 years apart to the day, and after three years of Drake being home with us, he had a baby brother.

My entrance into motherhood did not fit the timeline of everyone else on a normal path, nor did it meet my expected level of effort. It required our nonstop attention, like a full-time job before the child was even in the home. This path was a longer road than I expected. I stepped out in flip-flops, and I really should have packed hiking boots. God took me on quite the journey. If for some reason He asked me if I would do it this way again, I can honestly say I would. I'm glad that God chose this path for me, even if it wasn't normal.

Whether your title of "mom" was hard-won with emotional roller coasters, or a no-fuss, uncomplicated blessing, you are Mom. And every road, sidewalk, trail, and obstacle course that brought each mom here in a different way changes how she approaches the practice of motherhood. The circumstances we experience shape who we are, and the moms we will become.

ALL DIFFERENT, ALL MOM

Mothering is a sacred duty, it's not our entire identity. And despite all being called "Mom," the way we all live out this calling is very unique.[1] Individualized. Even our journeys *to* motherhood vary vastly. Our strengths and weaknesses are paired with the challenges and beauties of our families. God has given each us different dreams, and our individual personalities shine through our roles of mom in magnificently diverse ways.

We are different, and we are all Mom.

We had different childhoods and come from different backgrounds. We prioritize different things and dedicate our time to different engagements. Our families look different and we are all on different road maps on the spiritual highway of life.

We are different, yet we are all Mom.

Each mother grows into her calling and her kids' needs, meaning no box is one-size-fits-all. When we try to put the sacred role of motherhood in a box at all, we cheapen it. We do motherhood a disservice. That box might come in the shape of a book, article, conversation, picture, magazine, sermon, movie, podcast, or however else culture is communicated. The box itself is made up of flimsy, flaky material like assumptions, prejudices, unforgiveness, judgment, and arrogance. When we stereotype and micromanage what being a mom *should* look like, we risk making something beautiful sterile and cold.

Except, like most people, I tend to be a step-by-step "break it down for me" kind of person—which is precisely what these boxes promise to do. While I *think* I'd love a "Ten Steps to Effective Mom-ing" checklist, that would ultimately cheapen my calling. Listen closely now.

We need instruction, but not methods so specific that they squeeze individuality out completely.

We need guidance, not a mold.

We require principles, not a checklist.

In light of our individuality, there are some central concepts to being the darn-good mom that we seek so desperately to become. There are big-picture core ideas that apply to us all. Beautifully woven within all our diversity and individuality of motherhood,

When we

stereotype and

micromanage

what being a mom

should look like,

we risk making

something

beautiful sterile

and cold.

we follow consistent models and concepts. These are the ideologies that I believe we can all adopt into mothering without sacrificing or excluding the diversity of modern parenthood. There will always be differences, sure, but let's look at the similarities. Let's look at our common goal.

Unity is what brings the public-school mom and the homeschool mom together and say:

You got this!

That is what brings the married and single moms together to listen, learn, and say:

You got this!

That is what brings the younger and older moms together to grow and say:

You got this!

These common themes of joyful motherhood are for *all* mamas. If there is a child who calls you "Mom," this book is for you. We are gifted with instruction and research that provide wisdom in parenthood, not black-and-white answers. Instead of making an eighty-part encyclopedia covering everything on child and parent psychology, and instead of over-simplifying the complexities of modern circumstances surrounding what being a mom is all about, I want to get into the heart of our relationships with our kids, our relationship with God about being a mom, and our relationship with making mistakes. I've grown a little tired of either unpacking boxed versions of "Mom" or being told to just learn as I go.

LEARNING AS WE GROW

"Kids don't come with a manual; we are all just learning as we go."

Goodness…As a mom, you've probably had some version of it this past week. The "learning as we go" conversation comes as a response to many different concerns.

When we are conflicted about something parenting-related that has no right or wrong answer: "It will be fine—just trust your gut. You'll learn, and it will all work out."

When we feel defeated, maybe. We seek out a friend, frustrated and exhausted, look-ing for an ounce of hope that it gets easier: "Nobody gave me a playbook when I left the hospital. We were all in that boat at one time, but you learn one thing at a time."

It's possible you are tired and burnt-out right now. You are giving this motherhood thing all you've got, but no matter how much anyone says you can, you really don't think you can keep up anymore. You vent to your friend, who says you can: "I know it's hard. Learning and going at the same time is exhausting."

Maybe that dark Mom Guilt cloud has grabbed ahold of you. After confiding in a friend, she encourages you with: "Don't beat yourself up. Each kid is unique, and no child comes with a handbook. Each mother learns about her child and herself as she goes. Your child is learning as they go too. We are all just learning as we go."

Ladies who are perpetually learning on the go, you're in good company here. We'll spend some quality time on those really valid and painful feelings that often come with being a mom, but first, there's an elephant in the room: what we've been taught it means to learn, and what we've been taught it means to go.

You see, we've been led to believe some half-truths when it comes to time. Perhaps you're familiar with the old adage, "Time heals all wounds." If you (or someone you know) has stared grief in the face, you can attest that time does not really "heal" the hurt. The pain doesn't go away. We learn to grow around it and carry it. Time is not a magic wand, and these silly little comfort sayings can become crutches to our mindset and development when we look at them that way.

What we are technically doing when we use the phrase "learning as we go" is put-ting time on a shiny pedestal of power. We are giving time itself the credit to growth. We are ultimately lowering the measurement of growth to simply *remaining a mom.* If time is the metric of growth, we become better moms just by keeping the children alive. Certainly experience, which is gained through the passage of time, improves our ability, but that still requires the effort of using past mistakes as opportunities to learn and do something new next time. I'm sure there's a semantics debate in this somewhere, but here's *my* point:

We will never be able to wait the hard parts of motherhood out. We cannot assume that time itself will develop us into being the good mom that we all so desperately yearn to become. When the babies don't sleep through the night when everyone else's does, and when the toddler doesn't speak or enunciate as well as the others do, and when the young children aren't socializing or picking up skills that you need around the house,

We cannot assume that time itself will

develop us into being the good mom that

we all so desperately yearn to become.

and the tantrums are *every half hour,* the temptation and default setting is to just get through it. To just keep going.

But "just getting through this phase" or repeating what hasn't been working because you'd rather check out and get to the "good part" of motherhood is not what we're called to be, mamas. God asked us to step into this role alert and willing to be a part of every part. Being alert and present is a lot more strenuous when we try to resist, when we reinforce the bad habits and unsuccessful practices, or when we do what is easy even when it's not best for our kids.

When we chose to be mothers, God asked us to step in wholeheartedly, committed to every beautiful step in nurturing his children, and be willing to grow too.

If we want to be attentive moms, committed to raising our kids mindfully, the reality is we will be growing just as much as they do. Maybe not in height or shoe sizes, but in so many other important ways. This motherhood thing is the real deal. It takes more dedication, energy, and effort than anything I've ever committed myself to before.

We all know it's hard work. We all know it requires great effort and self-sacrifice. Time correlates with maturity—I'm not asking us to leave the delivery rooms with lesson plans for the next eighteen years. I'm telling you that I believe you are capable and made to raise your kid exactly how God wants you to *right now.*

We can accept that we don't know everything *and* we know a lot more than we think. The job description for parenting kids has no minimum number of years' experience required. It requires that we show up humble, grateful, and full of grace for ourselves and others.

Time isn't the central metric of whether we are really going to be better at this motherhood thing, be happier people, and rely on God. We learn as we go when we allow those things to grow us.

We're all meant to learn as we *grow.*

MY ROSE GARDEN

I recently began dabbling in the gardening world. I'm interested in growing fruits and veggies, but I'm also a girly girl, so, I like growing things that are pretty! For me, there is nothing more gorgeous than a rose garden.

A few years ago, I found a park that features an acre-long bed of roses. You can imagine this has become one of my favorite places! When I approach the flower beds, I can smell their aroma far before I even see their different-colored petals. There is nothing quite like it. I take pictures and examine them each one by one as I walk by. Their beauty is undeniable.

When I appreciate the beauty of the roses, I'm smelling them and looking at their hues, but ultimately the flower itself is just a byproduct of the stem. It's a result of the unbelievably tedious system of growth that occurred within the roots planted deep within the soil. I'm appreciating the delicate, fickle creation that took *years*.

Believe me, I tried to grow the same roses at home. That's exactly why I can appreciate their petals in the park all the more. I wanted to replicate what I saw, but I quickly realized that it takes top-notch soil to yield such breathtaking blooms.

To be the moms we want for our kids and for God's glory, it's going to take less focus on the pretty, up-close picture (and smell) on one magical sunny day, and more hands-on attention on our soil. It's where we are planted that makes all the difference. If we are planted in mediocre soil, we are going to get mediocre growth. We may have a rose bud or two, but we will not attain the results we are after.

Consequently, if we root ourselves in what God's Word has to say and research supports, we can grow a breathtaking bed of roses and provide a perfume-like aroma for our children's benefit. We will leave a scent of God's goodness and the beauty of motherhood in our path.

Try your best to keep that heart of yours open to uproot parts of your mothering that need replanting. That you would dedicate to be replanted in the *good soil*. The good soil is a place we can be rooted in God which will enable us to obey what He shares on how to do this thing called motherhood. My prayer is that you'd also see that there's some practical things we can begin to implement *today*.

I'm definitely after a gorgeous rose garden with beautiful blooms—all the reds, pinks, and whites! Maybe it's a different kind of flower for you. We're not in contest with each other either. We're in this together because each garden has amazing potential with the right soil, and we all want to leave a lasting impression on our children in the same way the rose garden made an impression on me. But are you ready to get your hands dirty? We are going to dig in the dirt and find some good soil to plant our roots and begin growing.

CHAPTER TWO

A Guarantee

n college, my friend used a black North Face backpack. She managed to fit many textbooks, a computer, a pencil bag, a notebook, and much more into the bag, even if it was too much weight for her back. Of course, such feats of strength were no match for gravity and sharp textbook edges, and a rip soon appeared. It was annoying, but unless it was rainy, the rip was not big enough to be a risk to anything in her backpack. I actually kind of giggled because she'd spent so much on a fancy backpack only for it to break within the first semester.

Then, a few days later, she sat down for class with the same backpack, but new. No rips, and yes, fewer textbooks.

"What did you do to it?" I asked.

"They give you a new one if your old one breaks during the lifetime of the backpack. Manufacturer's fault kind of thing. It's a Lifetime Guarantee the North Face does," she explained, smiling in relief.

I was impressed with North Face. It seemed nice to purchase a product knowing if it turns out to be a lemon, the company had a plan. They weren't going to give you the bag and receipt and abandon you if their coat, shoes, or whatever else was defective even beyond the return window.

It's super cool! But I'd love that for parenting. I'm not perfect, nor are my kids, and it'd be nice to know we're both guaranteed their lives and our relationship with them will stay healthy, safe, and God-focused. How do I get a Lifetime Warranty on parenthood? That my children will always be Jesus followers who make good choices and stay out of trouble? I hoped God would have me covered on that.

THE "GUARANTEE"

Moms want the guarantee that if something goes wrong, it'll get fixed. That things will be okay. I wouldn't say I was completely naïve. I knew life brought hardships and struggles; *that* I expected. What I desperately sought out was the guarantee, the warranty; I sought an assurance similar to the one the North Face offered. I wanted to be assured that after my children went through their "difficult seasons," they would be okay in the end. Just like the backpack, even if life roughed them up a bit, there was always a guaranteed solution awaiting.

At this point, if you "know your Bible," you may be thinking, "God does gives us a guarantee!" Haven't you heard of that lovely (and often-quoted) Bible verse that says that if you raise your child to love Jesus, they will turn out right? Okay, I may be paraphrasing here. The actual verse goes like this:

> *"Train up a child in the way he should go;*
> *Even when he is old, he will not depart from it."*
> **Proverbs 22:6**

I had more than one experience where this verse was thrown out as a guarantee. Everything in the Bible is God's inspired words, which means this could be considered a promise…right?

When a mom is desperate for assurance, this is the "pocket verse" sometimes shared. [2] I think deep down even the person who is quoting the verse doesn't truly believe it is a guarantee. We just so desperately long for a one, though, that we begin to whip out memorable verses and "pretty them up" to make it sound like it's the solution. Sometimes it *sounds good,* so we just go with it.

We mean well. Honest to goodness, I know I have done this before too. I hear of a mom who is struggling and my mind begins to imaginatively flip the pages of Scripture to find the *perfect verse* she needs to hear. We so badly wish we could solve their issue with Scripture. We know that God provides hope, so we then just insert a verse that *sounds* like a promise. Resting in the unknown is hard, so we err on the side of "filling in the blanks" for God at times.

Yet, I think we could agree that this "plug and chug" method of sharing God's truth will never fill our heart's desire for assurance. I know for me personally, I hung onto this Proverbs "promise" for a while. I meditated on it and convinced myself of its protection.

No matter how long I meditated on that verse, nor how tightly I clung on to it as my backpack guarantee, it never quite settled with me, though. I knew I couldn't have such a guarantee.

It was time to process the gravity of this motherhood thing. The responsibility is too great for me not to take seriously. I wanted to know exactly why that Proverb was mentioned, what God had to say about motherhood, and how it all applied to my life specifically. Though it was easier and simpler, I let go of the interpretations I *wanted* verses to mean and dedicated myself to examine context and God's character more. I was prepared to learn the big-picture answers God had for me and for us, even if it wasn't what I initially believed or wanted to be true. God is good, so even if the answer didn't feel good in the moment, even if it wasn't a guarantee waiting for me on the other side, God still designed motherhood to be good. Peace could still be had, even in the midst of the unknown.

MAMA OVERDRIVE

The book of Proverbs is a collection of God's wisdom. When we read what God has to say about many experiences in life, we learn how to navigate those experiences with godly discernment. It's almost that "talk with your grandparent" concept. They've been through all that life has to offer, and they are sharing some tidbits of wisdom to help you along the way. Now, God Himself is wisdom, and here He is in Proverbs giving us nugget after nugget of that wisdom to digest. He's giving us a guide on how to live life with discernment, not a collection of "yes" and "no" assurances.

Proverbs aren't promises. Yep, you heard me right. The statements in Proverbs are actually not meant to be guarantees at all. What you read in Proverbs are not transactional statements where I do X and God will grant me Y for my good effort. If you think about it, that's a works-based relationship right there. That is a self-righteous perspective. There's plenty of Proverbs that we understand are principles and not guarantees.

The wisdom we read in the book of Proverbs are generally true, not universally true. They're intended to grow our ability to perceive situations, follow God, and stay encouraged.

Take Proverbs 15:1, for example. It says, *"A soft answer turns away wrath, but a harsh word stirs up anger."* Now, generally speaking, a soft answer would be the best course of action because if you address a sticky situation with a calm voice and clear head, that will generally be more easily accepted by the listener. That is great wisdom given to us

I was prepared to learn the big-picture answers

God had for me and for us, even if it wasn't what

I initially believed or wanted to be true.

by the Lord. This isn't a guarantee, though. We aren't preaching that as long as you are kind and understanding toward others, you will never be subject to wrath. No, that would be silly. We can't guarantee that.

Why do we sometimes twist these verses into guarantees, then? Because we want one!

Prior to my relinquished control, my response was to swing fervently into action. I read everything I could get my hands on. I scrolled social media at night reading inspirational quotes. I subscribed to all the best blogs. I went on Pinterest to plan the perfect afternoon. I was all-hands-on deck because I thought that was *the answer*. I thought, "If I could just do more, I could be better. If I could just be better, then I will be one step closer to my guarantee, right?"

This "Mama Overdrive" bit quickly got out of hand. I was fooling myself into believing if I could be as Christian as possible, my children would ultimately be Christians too, *guaranteed*. While I believed intellectually in God's sovereignty, my actions were not aligning with my belief patterns as I felt compelled to add on all the other "good stuff" to overcompensate and ultimately add coins to my bank of assurance.

I did this in many ways. I had a schedule for everything. I was deeply studying every TV show prior to giving the kids approval to watch. I would read about preventing sudden infant death syndrome (SIDS). I was learning about supplements and vitamins, trying to comprehend the benefits of each. (I am still totally clueless about that one, by the way.) I was at the library checking out books in every academic area to provide exposure. All the while, I was wearing myself absolutely thin. I was actually getting sick rather than staying healthy. I was putting the world on my shoulders and doing it all in the name of being a "good mom." In all actuality, I think I needed to let go, get on the floor, and play some more.

It would be a different story if I was doing those things out of overflow of conviction or calling. But I wasn't. I was being self-righteous. If you pulled back the layers of my heart, you'd find a mom who was not willing to trust anyone with the gift God gave her. I waited so long to be "Mom," and now that I had my babies, I wasn't letting go. The sad part was, I wasn't even willing to trust the Lord with them. He gave them to me, yet I was stubbornly squeezing them onto my sides. I wasn't giving in. I wasn't willing to trust God without a warranty.

That's not a sustainable way to live. After I cracked from the pressure of *doing* motherhood "right," I then swung the other way. I figured that what was going to happen would happen. I became apathetic and threw my hands in the air. When I realized I couldn't have a guarantee in the sense that I wanted, I felt like I lost the war. I wasn't going to submit to this trust thing; I was just going to give up completely. I felt hopeless. I fooled myself into thinking that if God *really* loved me and my children, He would ultimately work everything out. I didn't really have to put the hard work in because at the end of the day, it didn't seem like it really made a difference anyway. I thought, "As long as I have good intentions, everything will fall into place." I'd compare myself to other moms, and they didn't seem as stressed out about this guarantee thing like I was. Maybe the answer was to stop caring so much. So that is exactly what I did.

This way of thinking was so opposite of my personality, I found that I was no longer able to sleep. The guilt ate me up inside. I wasn't being my best and I knew it. I tried to fill my guilt with other things to justify why my time was dedicated elsewhere. I saw *real results* in the other areas I put my time. In some cases, what I was dedicating my time toward actually had a guarantee, like an award, paycheck, or title. I wanted so desperately to settle for this mediocre motherhood, but the guilt just wouldn't leave me alone. I was miserable.

Deep down, I knew neither side of the coin was the answer. I'm sure that comes to no surprise. But coming to that conclusion brings some level of hopelessness. Knowing you have no true assurance in motherhood brings on feelings of depression and panic. I felt stuck.

OUR FATHER'S CHILD

The further into motherhood we journey, the more we realize we really are still the child. We are called *God's* children. We've heard the saying, "kids will be kids." It means children are developing, it's a process, and some things are just the way they are. Just as your child may currently be in the process of learning how to tie their shoes or working up the courage to go on their first sleepover, we too are in-process. There are many processes at work, but one of them is the process to trust.

God has gifted you with this precious child. A child that you love beyond what words can describe. Yet, you realize you do not have control over how your child responds to your parenting. You have to simply guide, lead, and show them the way to go. You must point them toward the path you wish for them to take. The path you know is safe, right, and true.

God takes us on a similar journey. He wishes that you'd trust Him. In the same way He simply guides, leads, and shows you the way to go, He hopes you choose His path, but He won't make that decision for you. The best thing He can do as a parent is show His kids the path is safe, right, and true.

You can grab continuously for your Proverbs 22:6 guarantee as long as you need—doing everything you believe the verse implies is needed to train them up in the right way. Even when we know the verse isn't a promise in our heads, it's hard to accept in our hearts. But whenever you're ready, embrace that verse for what it is: wisdom. Then focus all of that energy not in controlling your kid but by trusting your heavenly Father.

Every mom longs for the normal, predictable path when it comes to her child's development, but sometimes beautiful things happen in the unknowns, unexpected, or unplanned. But even when it's hard, we do have promises in other places of the Bible from God:

> *"It is the LORD who goes before you. He will be with you;*
> *he will not leave you or forsake you. Do not fear or be dismayed."*
> **DEUTERONOMY 31:8**

> *"…for those who love God, all things work together for good,*
> *for those who are called according to his purpose."*
> **ROMANS 8:28**

I don't know how it all works together. I have no guarantee. I'm here to tell you, though, that He's *bigger* than your guarantee.

WORTH A THOUSAND WORDS

I remember after Drake came home, we went on vacation relatively soon afterward. We traveled to Arizona, which is my happy place. The red clay and green cactus make my heart glow warmer than the sun that shines there. I scheduled a photographer to take pictures of our new family on our trip. It meant a lot to me. I had high expectations, and I owned it. I remember contacting the photographer and specifically requesting all sorts of poses and backgrounds. I made sure they knew how big of a deal this was. We waited years for our son, and he was now here. We could now take pictures for the first time *together* as a family. These pictures would be priceless to me.

When arriving to meet them at the park, the photographer hadn't brought the list of

Every mom longs for the normal,

predictable path when it comes to

her child's development, but

sometimes beautiful things happen

in the unknowns, unexpected, or

unplanned.

poses I requested. They didn't seem to understand the importance of this. At one point, I remember being stern and insisting they do the poses I envisioned.

The photographer politely nodded and continued to ignore my requests. She told us to walk and play. She promised me the pictures would be beautiful.

When I opened the pictures the week after arriving back home, they were breathtaking. The sun was setting behind the cactus, and there was the family that God brought together, laughing, smiling, and enjoying the gift of each other. The photos were not done in the way I imagined, and I couldn't have been any more grateful.

The photographer clearly knew best. I thought I knew what I wanted from the experience, but while patient, the photographer knew that wasn't the best course of action—and that in all honesty, the poses I'd planned looked silly—and steered us in a new direction. But I didn't know it until I saw them. I knew she was the pro and she told me to trust her, but I had a hard time doing that. And I didn't love every picture—not for artistry reasons but for maybe my own insecurities or concerns. But the album was beautiful. She nailed it.

Ephesians 3:20 tells us that God is capable to do far more abundant things than we can even dream. Paul tells us we can't even ask or think it. So, when you are desperate for *that thing* to happen or not to happen to your child, that means that God has ever greater things in mind! Things you can't even imagine.

God knows what He's doing. He is the *professional,* as you will. He has crafted together beautiful stories from the beginning of time, and I don't believe we've even experienced His best work yet! I can't wait until I get to heaven and understand more of His plans, ways, and masterful storytelling.

ZEBEDEE'S MOTHER OF TWO

God has woven some pretty incredible stories. He has worked in people's lives to model for us time and time again how He can work all things out for our good and His glory, even when the circumstances appear bleak. Even when we (or our kids) don't take the path we envisioned. Even when we can't envision how the story will end.

There is nothing wrong with dreaming. There is nothing wrong with preparation for the future and making plans. The plans just have to be flexible and open. Otherwise, when we show up with our list of demands in the same way I showed up to that photoshoot, we're shocked God didn't get the poses. God's plan always surpasses ours.

Despite all that we do to have a hand in the outcome and future of our children's lives, the Lord has the final say.

> *"We humans keep brainstorming options and plans,*
> *but God's purpose prevails."*
> **PROVERBS 19:21 MSG**

When motherhood inevitably gives way to difficulty, I sometimes shake my fist at God and ask some accusatory questions. Why did You allow this to happen? Why can't it be easier for us after all we've done to serve You? Ultimately God doesn't answer to us, and He sees behind the camera. He's building character and growing our faith in Him.

This growing business isn't anything new. Mothers have been learning as they grow for centuries. Take the disciple James and John's mother for instance:

> *"Then the mother of the sons of Zebedee came up to [Jesus] with her*
> *sons, and kneeling before him she asked him for something. And he said*
> *to her, 'What do you want?' She said to him, 'Say that these two sons*
> *of mine are to sit, one at your right hand and one at your left, in your*
> *kingdom.' Jesus answered, 'You do not know what you are asking.'"*
> **MATTHEW 20:20-22**

As a mom of two boys, I laugh out loud when reading this! I can totally relate. This sweet mama just wants her sons to be honored. In a sense, we probably all have prayed something very similar to this.

"Please Lord, grant my children abundance, blessing, and honor."

After all, our dreams are so great—our ambitions for our children sky-high. How could we refrain from bringing such a request to Jesus? I love the answer, though. How Jesus responds to this mother is so kind.

Jesus tells this mother, "You do not know what you are asking." He doesn't condemn, and I bet He had a little snicker on his face when he said it. He knows her heart. She is just a mother who just really, *really* loves her boys! Jesus just knows that's not the plan, though. That is not the end of the story He's written.

I have found that God gives me what is needed over what is desirable. We most likely will never know the details of the *why* behind the story God's writing for our lives. He's not expecting us to understand why all at once or even at all. What He's asking is for trust.

Maybe you are sharing your list with the Lord like I did with the photographer. You have the plans for your children all written out and keep trying to hand it to Him despite Him not taking it. Are you James and John's proud mother asking the Lord for some pretty hefty guarantees? I promise you, God is listening. He is smiling at you and sees your heart. He actually really loves that you are honest and are sharing those with Him.

He doesn't want you to worry, though. He's probably not going to give you that guarantee, but He does promise that He hasn't forgotten, nor will He ever forget about either you or your children. As we make our way through life, God is taking some pretty incredible snapshots. I can *guarantee* you'll be amazed when you see the final product.

CHAPTER THREE

Heart Overflows

Heart Ovations

My husband can't resist joking with me. Every time I eat a peach, I go into the stories of my family's peach trees. The stories usually start with, "This reminds me of my childhood. I grew up growing peaches…" He doesn't let me live in down. Being married thirteen years now, he can recall all of my peach stories. It's hard to resist telling them though whenever I bite into a sweet peach.

Since you haven't heard them yet, I'll share one peach memory. I grew up around peaches. Funny enough, my parents then eventually moved to the "Peach Capital of the World," a small town in South Carolina. They just seem to have always been in my family. I remember as a girl blanching the peaches in the kitchen and canning all the *fruits of our labor*. It's not a job for the impatient. You plant the seed and tend to it for *years* before the tree bears fruit, then you pick that golden baby off with a smile and finally get to take that juicy bite.

Not all of our peaches were good, though. There were times the tree would die, the peaches would be zapped by frost, or sadly—when the branches were too heavy or uneven—they would sometimes break off, causing the peaches on that limb to perish. The peaches were only as good as the tree was healthy. If the tree was bad, the peaches would be bad as well.

If you want tasty peaches, you start with a healthy peach tree. The more you care for the tree, the better tasting your peaches will be. The better soil you plant your tree in, the healthier it will become, ensuring those healthy peaches will arrive.

THE PEACH SHOULDN'T
FALL FAR FROM THE TREE

The peach trees remind me of when we hear little babies or toddlers say something inappropriate. Some adults think this is just hilarious—I'm not going to pretend it's never made me laugh. But we all know they learned the phrase not in a dictionary or book but from their parents and general environment.

Even the words we don't *direct* at our kids reach their ears and burrow in their minds—which is so darn ironic when our specific, clear instructions hardly ever seem to. Everything we say, how we say it, when we say it, how consistently we say it, and why we say it affects their growth and development. We might not realize it until we "bite into the peach" or hear them say something we didn't realize they picked up on or felt.

Learning the right mother-child communication style for situations is a valuable way we can build strong connections with our kids. Not only will we feel more heard (in the way we want), but they will too. God talks about this very thing, and how the answer to communicating better with our children begins in the heart. Just as the peaches begin with the soil the tree is planted in, our communication begins with our heart.

> *"Either make the tree good and its fruit good, or make the tree bad and its fruit bad, for the tree is known by its fruit. You brood of vipers! How can you speak good, when you are evil? For out of the abundance of the heart the mouth speaks. The good person out of his good treasure brings forth good, and the evil person out of his evil treasure brings forth evil."*
>
> MATTHEW 12:33-36

Jesus was talking to the Pharisees—men who believed themselves to be the holiest of all, really good at following Moses' Law, yet in the Bible, often got mixed up about actually *following* God. In this passage, the Pharisees associated a miracle of Jesus with Satan, which was a grave sin. Their words and actions toward Jesus revealed their true intentions and heart. Jesus rebuked them, reminding them everything we do stems from the heart.

Everything overflows from the heart. Whatever we have tucked away inside of us, whatever we find deep within our souls, will ultimately be reflective in the words that we say and the way we interact with our children. The Pharisees were kidding themselves if they believed that good could come out of a rotten heart.

Just as the peaches begin with the soil the

tree is planted in, our communication

begins with our heart.

For our children, being the best moms we can be means committing to grow our heart in good soil, to produce good peaches (or whatever fruit you like!), and *demonstrate* what our words say we mean. I have compiled three *heart overflows* that we can identify within ourselves and begin integrating in our relationships with our kids.

EMPATHETIC ENCOURAGER

This is the mom who understands that the world can sometimes be a cruel place, and in order to maintain their child's innocence, joy, and sweet spirit, they are going to need a double dose of edifying words. This heart overflow recognizes that we must first embody a state of empathy for our children.

To define our terms further, empathy in motherhood means doing our best to put ourselves in the mindset, emotions, and situations of someone else with the intention of understanding and relating with them. Our children will experience emotions and have thoughts that are not our own—ones that we may not even understand or agree with at times—but that we can still be present and offer support for.

For the preschooler, that may mean their balloon popped, and their world is crumbling because of it. That was their special prize, and in their heads, it's the only balloon in the world. For the teenager, empathizing might mean stepping into the out-of-fashion shoes you wore at their age to understand how they feel when they were not invited to the party and fear they're an outcast.

The circumstances change as they age, but our commitment to empathize should remain. Our children will experience a wide range of emotions throughout their day as they encounter the world. Together, let's put on the glasses that view these as opportunities, not inconveniences, annoyances, or jokes. We can use these emotions to have great conversations that have depth and value (and *then* giggle in private about funny reasons for toddler tantrums or middle school sass). We can use these emotions as an opportunity to connect with them relationally and build a deep bond. Even when the emotions seem silly, unwarranted, or misplaced, we should be leaning in and not backing up or invalidating.

Emotions are typically easier to recognize and identify in our children, but empathizing also relates to our children's thoughts. These are what we call in behavior analysis "private events." As a behavior therapist, I work mostly with cognitive behavior therapy (CBT), which in a nutshell centers around the premise that our thoughts and emotions *together* drive our actions.[3]

We are a lot better at recognizing outward emotions because they are visible. It takes less awareness. For instance, if our child is sad, we will often recognize this sooner if they cry rather than sulk. If our children are feeling angry, we will notice this if they begin to yell quicker than if they just stew or hide. Thoughts can be easily missed. They are not acting upon them (yet), so we do not yet know the problem is present. The key to unlocking our child's thoughts is by intentionally asking depth-filled questions. These can be questions about anything that initiates a two-way conversation. Conversation is what reveals your child's internal context and processing on a deeper level before it emerges within their emotions. Or even if they have an emotional response (which is okay, just more noticeable), conversation is what allows us to peel back the layers to determine what is truly occurring, not just what it looks like.

To get a two-way conversation going, keep questions open-ended yet guided. What I mean by that is we cannot allow the question to be so broad that they do not know what we'd like out of the conversation. Examples of these are the famous, "How was your day?" but also the commonly used question, "How are you doing?" They're too broad, and our children often avoid them or give superficial answers because the full answer to that is really hard to think of on the spot or even recognize.

Instead, zero in a bit more, still leaving room for interpretation. Some better questions to provoke a depth-filled conversation would include, "What is something that I do that makes you feel loved?" or "How can I help you after school?" Questions like these will ultimately lead to a conversation with feedback or at least a response, and it's narrow enough for children to understand what is expected of them to a degree.

I'll let you in on a secret: your children love talking to you! Yes, even when they are older and say you're not cool anymore. Asking them open-ended, depth-filled questions gets our children talking, which will in return give us insight into their *thought life*. These questions can be anything from the silly "Would You Rather" game, gathering their insight on a current event, or simply asking for their opinion on a topic. Moving from reflex questions ("how was your day?") to depth-filled questions is like a muscle. The more you work it, the stronger and easier it will become.

Being a mom who embodies empathy involves intentional recognition of our children's emotions and thoughts. That is the launchpad into being an *Empathetic Encourager*. You see, we cannot truly be encouraging to our children unless it is rooted in empathy. If we focus first on encouragement, it often ends up hollow, superficial, and forced. Consequently, if you begin with empathy, encouragement will naturally flow.

One reason I feel our children crave this empathy and encouragement from us so much is because the world continues to grow colder and crueler. Unfortunately, while we desperately wish we could shield our children from the effects that sin has had on our world, it's unavoidable. They will be exposed to some degree of selfishness, rudeness, bullying, or mistreatment from the peers and environments they come into contact with.[4] I know this breaks your heart because it breaks mine. Whenever my sons are exposed to something that I don't approve of, it's upsetting. It's easy to stay in a place of hopelessness, but there actually is a lot of hope found in these unfortunate times.

When our children come home, we can make it a place of refuge. We cannot control others. While we so badly wish we could, we cannot always control their environment, exposures, or experiences. What we do have a choice in, though, is what occurs in our home. How are we responding?

Our words to our kids aren't meant for nagging, complaining, and almost whining. Use them to welcome your kids' emotions and thoughts through meaningful talks. Use them to build them up out of a place of relation. With time, we create a safe space even when the world becomes dark, allowing for them to feel comfortable talking with us about everything, even things of great depth.

BACK-SEAT CONVERSATIONALIST

The *Back-Seat Conversationalist* is the mama who forfeits her right to be in charge, instead allowing her child to take the driver's seat in the conversation. This is the mom who recognizes that communicating with her child is extremely important, but that it needs a back-and-forth exchange. This mom values what her child has to share and their perspective.

One of the hats I wear in my profession is a "parent consultant." When I have the opportunity to consult with parents, I always begin by establishing that I believe they are good parent. I've never had a parent reach out to me who wasn't a good parent. Asking for help is strong. Always striving to be better through healthy paths is admirable. We all need that.

When it comes to meaningful talks with our kids, though, we want to drive the car. We know what's best. We have subjects that mean a lot to us. There's plenty we want to know about our kids! We also don't have time for things that are "not important," right? Even harder, what our children find conversation-worthy is the direct opposite of our own agendas, or seem quite pointless.

You might sit down to read a story and make it not one page before your child has several questions completely unrelated to the book. You ask what they want for dinner, and they tell you about a friend's new toy. You ask how their day was at school, and they ask you in return about the family's plans next weekend. It's almost frustrating at times. If you're like me, you want to step in and correct this. "*That's not what I asked you,*" you may want to respond. *Did they hear anything I said?* you may wonder.

Taking the back seat is giving up the right to be in control of the conversation. After all, we typically are engaging in this type of conversation to connect with them. If that truly is our goal, does it have to be on our terms? How are we to determine what is important? If the goal is to connect, then connect on their terms.

Jesus provides a special form of taking the back seat for us when He used parables to communicate a message. His messages in these parables were highly important concepts. They are concepts we absolutely need to understand. Yet, He didn't just say what the parables meant (apart from His disciples I suppose), or skip to the moral of the story and skip the parables at all. Jesus was not demanding that He steer the communication ship. He was encouraging conversation, no matter where it led or what was on the people's hearts. The parables were intended to draw out questions, to initiate deeper thought, and to hear what others thought He was saying so He could get to know them better. The communication method Jesus used within these parables doesn't minimize the message; rather, it allows for inquiry and a two-way conversation to take place.

On an average day, there are many interactions when our form of communication and our words need to trump theirs—perhaps for efficiency and clarity. You are asking for them to complete things (Can you let out the dog?), correcting them on something (Please don't touch that), and reminding them of expectations (Remember you need to be home by nine p.m.). Most of our communication to them is instructional where we are in the driver's seat. Our authority requires this type of direction and leadership.

When we find those moments when we don't *need* to have a conversational agenda, let's throw being in control aside. Let's start a conversation and then let our kids determine where it goes. I bet you'll be surprised how you will connect with ease. You will also be blessed! As you grow closer with your child, you get to discover what makes them tick. Just as the disciples came to ask Jesus about the parables' meaning, I think we'd be pleasantly surprised how often our children will begin seeking us out with questions when we adopt this communication style.

The Back-Seat Conversationalist doesn't just allow the child to lead the conversation, but they recognize that a conversation is a back-and-forth exchange.

The trick is to also stay engaged and participate enough to avoid a one-sided conversation where the child does all the talking. We've all been there. This is where our child is rambling or knee-deep into a story, but we are simply responding *"uh-huh, yep, ah, oh."* We say just enough to keep the conversation train on the tracks, but we are not adding anything of value. That's not being present or truly invested. We could always find a way to jump in and participate (even when we've heard the story about how their blue truck is the fastest ten times today).

My favorite way to do this is to jump in with something humorous that will cause a rebuttal: "Oh yeah? Well, I bet my spaceship is so fast that it can take your blue truck, fly it around the moon, and bring it back all in ten minutes." Usually, I get a twinkle in their eye with excitement that I was willing to jump into their imaginative world. Their rebuttal usually begins, "Well, well, um…well…" as they think of how to combat the wrench I threw into their story. It allows me to engage with them in a fun way while not losing my marbles.

The sad reality is that often our children are so excited that we are "listening," they will not expect or ask us for more than superficial form of engagement. They will settle for the *"uh-huh, yep, ah, oh"* responses because it's better than nothing at all.

The content of the conversation doesn't dictate its importance. Even when it doesn't seem important, we know that *our children* are important. We can jump in simply because of who they are. Have fun with it!

GRACE-GIVING REALIST

You may say, "I just get so burnt out, though." Well, that leads us right into our third persona, which is the *Grace-Giving Realist.* There needs to be a balance in motherhood. Growing is never a perfect upward trajectory. We get tired and take breaks; we mess up and need to make amends; we get confused and need instructions; or we get lost and have to recalibrate. We can't do it without a lot of grace, patience, forgiveness, and understanding for ourselves.

I like to think of the Grace-Giving Realist as the mom who gives her best effort during the day and forgives herself when her head hits the pillow that she didn't do it perfectly. She recognizes that God made this beautiful child, and out of everyone in the world,

The content of the conversation doesn't dictate its importance. Even when it doesn't seem important, we know that our children are important.

He chose her to be their mama. She feels the weight of that wonderful responsibility, but doesn't fret. She believes that through the Holy Spirit, she can do the job, no matter how imperfect it may be completed. This mom believes that perfection isn't what God or her children are seeking from her. She is loved and valued as she is. She continues to show up and allows God to use her in both the highs and the lows. She has a confidence that radiates despite her imperfections.

Mamas struggle often with intense feelings of guilt, and they're exhausted by these intense feelings of guilt. They do not give themselves any room for grace, and in return, they feel miserable in motherhood. Mom guilt is a real thing experienced by practically every mother at times. For me personally, it's the overwhelming gravity of failure that creeps in. It begins when I get stuck in a sand-trap of labels: I messed up one time, but in my guilt-ridden brain, it becomes a character trait. Suddenly, I am labeled a failure. I know this isn't fair. I'd never put that on anyone else! A one-time mess up shouldn't equate me being a failure, but that is where my mind jumps if I'm not disciplined. If I'm not practicing the heart posture of a Grace-Giving Realist.

I fear that I'm a "bad mom." Did you shudder a bit? I think I can speak for most moms when they say being labeled a "bad mom" is their worst fear. This fear allows us to avoid that outcome at all costs. Hence, when we mess up, we feel an overwhelming sensation of guilt. We don't want to be the "bad mom" and when we (inevitably) mess up, we are overwhelmed that, in our heads, it could actually be true.

If we are really honest with one another, some of us feel so guilty when we try that we don't really want to try anymore. If we are going to mess up either way, might as well put forth the minimum amount of effort. In the hidden parts of our souls, I'm sure I'm not alone in these dark thoughts of discontentment.

Discontentment comes from both comparing, and from holding ourselves to an unrealistic standard. Comparisons and unrealistic standards are like two sides of a coin. It can happen one of two ways. We compare ourselves, trying to match whatever we see done by those we care about no matter how different the context. Or we may *start* with unrealistic expectations before even *seeing* what anyone else is doing. We have read the books, seen the videos, attended the classes, bookmarked the recipes, set the bar sky-high, and consider anything less than that is a failure.

But "Mom" is as unique to us as our DNA, and grace is as necessary to life as oxygen.

I'm not sure how many of you have dogs, but if you've ever loved and owned one, perhaps you've accidentally wronged them—forgotten to feed them, came home late to let them out, or worst of all—stepped on their paw! We have no way of communicating to our dogs (in their "language") that we're sorry or that it wasn't intentional. Still, they recover and welcome us with undeserved affection and love us all the same—unable to tell us in any other way that they forgive us. Even when we can't shake the feeling of guilt from our little mistakes that day, remind yourself no one's keeping score. You're forgiven, and forgive yourself.

The antidote to comparison is grace. It's a free, unlimited antidote we have a hard time accepting because it seems like no one else wants to take it, but Jesus constantly reminds us there's no "catch." His forgiveness, our kids' forgiveness, and the forgiveness we can give ourselves comes with no penalty or limit.

Whether you start with unrealistic expectations that lead to comparisons or vice versa, they can easily paint motherhood to require this best-case scenario of constant intellectual, emotional, and spiritually rich and fulfilling experiences. It's unrealistic!

I'm sure you've heard this, but I want to say it again and again (because I know I need plenty of reminders each day). We cannot be "on" all of the time. Yes, you heard that right. You cannot always be everything to your kids. God has gifted us with some super-powers. We can do multiple things as the same time, we have eyes in the back of our head, and we can guess what move our child will take next. What we cannot do, though, is be present and available in every moment.

You need to take breaks. If nothing else, at least to go to the bathroom with the door closed. It's good for your children to see you taking a break. Rest is good. Alone time is good. Self-exploration is good. Please do not buy the lie that the *good moms* are the ones that don't hit pause and never take time for themselves. Don't believe the lie that the *good Moms* are the ones who plan activities despite wearing themselves thin.

Extending God's grace to ourselves might mean stopping negative self-talk as soon as we recognize it. It's giving ourselves some slack when you are trying to juggle an impossible wide load of responsibility. It's taking your own advice and lowering the standards you set for yourself. The sheer fact that being a "bad mom" scares you to the core is assurance that you are one darn-good mama! You do not need to continually beat yourself up or exhaust yourself trying to measure up.

You can do less, which I assure you will lead to being *more*. You will be more available, more pleasant, and more of what your children need when you become a realist. By saying *no more* to overbooking yourself, you may then find the energy needed to say *yes* to more to the things that you feel called to. You cannot be everything. You cannot do everything, either. But you can decide to be a Grace-Giving Realist. You can give yourself permission not be perfect, not to be "on" all the time, because ultimately, that's being real.

PRACTICE WHAT YOU PEACH

Did you know I grew up growing peaches? I remember this one day…No, but seriously, just like the peaches require their tree be planted in good soil, our hearts need to be planted in reality. Good soil does not overidealize and overdemand of moms. We can say "no" sometimes, and all in the world will be okay. It's better to be a kind and patient mom than one who *does everything* and ends up yelling or dragging herself through.

I'd highly encourage you to pick one or two things and do them *well.* Don't take on everything and do them halfway. If you are like me, you'll easily feel defeated and out of control. Give yourself *grace* that you can do less, and give them all you've got! You can start with anything: making dinner each night, limiting screen time, playing with them when they bathe—I mean, anything! Then give it all you've got, and give yourself grace that you'll work on something else next week.

And yes—that is *okay!*

I think every parenting book in the history of parenting books mentions something about how we need to communicate better with our children. We care about it, believe it is important, and some of us try really hard to do it right.

We also have some pretty impressive skill sets in the area of communicating. There is something to be said about a mom's multitasking skills of cooking dinner, talking on the phone, and still being able to answer their child's question about where you put their bookbag. Or simply how many words a day a woman is capable of using. Or the mom superpower to detect lies. Should I go on?

Even when we're on the same page, though, we can forget why.

Sure, we communicate. We use lots of words. We share what needs to be shared, and we articulate what needs to be said to get through the day effectively. We share the calendar of events, we remind our children of expectations, and on top of it all, we still have one-on-one conversations about the small (yet important) things.

The ultimate goal of communicating well is to foster deep, strong connection with our children. A relationship with your child that allows for them not only to hear but also feel secure in your love.

Trying to do any of what we talked about without understanding why will foolishly reveal what's really overflowing in our hearts: our own vanity and fear of being bad parents. We risk the confusion of the Pharisees, attempting to bring good out of something wicked. The connection that comes from communicating will be lost because it's not something we can fake our way through.

Root your peach tree, your bond with your child, in fertile soil. The kind that nurtures genuine interest and undistracted love beyond just wanting to do what is right or even having the skills to do something right.

If we desire a communication that builds connection, then we will need a heart that is right, which Psalm 119 sings about so beautifully as being connected to the Lord. God Himself represents this as He longs to move beyond simply telling us things to actually participating in a loving relationship. He doesn't desire that we regurgitate what we know of Him and robotically obey, either. He's after our hearts. A heart overflow, if you will, that results in love-driven action as a result of the communication we have with Him through His Word.

These "heart overflows" are just silly personas that I've created. They are not actual terms and are not published anywhere in literature (yet!). The goal of making them is just to improve how we interact with our kids in the appropriate contexts.

When you get home after dropping your kid off somewhere and realize you drove the car in a conversation your kid could have, remind yourself it takes time and grace. When you're brushing your teeth one night and it hits you maybe the "tough guy" was the wrong approach to your third-grader's bedtime wallows, take a deep breath and move forward. Tomorrow is a new day, you are already forgiven, and you can tell her you're sorry in the morning.

Did you know that a peach tree can take up to five years before producing its first fruit? The work is long, tedious, and painstaking at times. Oh, but I can assure you, there is nothing quite that sweet, rosy-orange reward. Each one is so precious, I'd admire them like works of art. The fruit of my family's labor.

CHAPTER FOUR

God and the Bumblebees

t was a home run. This day was really one for the books. I was feeling great—almost cocky if I'm honest. It was the first day of summer break. I had both my nine-year-old niece and my five-year-old son. I stayed up late the night before making their Bible study books. Each had their own personally Jenna-designed cover, including their favorite colors and names. Since there was an age gap, I also created two separate programs completely from scratch. Each would be watching a video and going through questions that I typed up specifically for them each week. It was colorful. It was fun. It was thoughtful.

Ten points, I secretly thought. *Add those points to your Mama Bank of good deeds.*

The day continued on as they were completely digging all the fun content I had planned! I introduced a Bible verse song followed by a craft.

Five points. You're really nailing this!

It wasn't long before they said they were hungry. I went into the kitchen and emerged with a huge peanut butter dipping platter on a trendy, lemon-decorated tray. Dig in, kids!

Give yourself ten more points, I thought. *This day truly is quite swell. I can do this summer-break thing.*

The day's itinerary also included going to the splash pad after we finished our Bible study lesson. Sadly though, when snack time was finished, it began to storm outside. I didn't panic though. I transitioned like a champ and created a glow-in-the-dark bath for them to play in! Bubbles galore. I covered the windows to make it extra dark. It was like swimming in a rainbow. I took a picture of them having a blast and sent it in the family group chat.

> *Okay, Jenna, I think you deserve twenty points for this one. You really outdid yourself to save this rainy day!*

At one point when throwing in bath toys for them to explore with, my son told me, "This is even better than the splash pad!"

I smiled and nodded my head. At that point, I'm not even sure I was happy they were having fun. I was just so smitten with myself for providing the perfect summer day.

It was eventually time for bed, and as I laid down with my son, he leaned over and asked, "Can Daddy put me to sleep? I love Daddy more than I love you."

I was caught off guard. My heart sank.

What was my response?

You better believe I bawled like a baby!

I was angry. I was overwhelmed. I was insecure. I felt like a bull rider, once riding like a champ but now sucking for air, bucked to the ground. I was just kicked off the bull and had the wind knocked out of me. I once was hearing the cheers, but now I was stuck alone in the mud, defeated.

A lot of the sting was amplified by the great day we'd had that somehow didn't factor into his request, but there's never a fun time to hear that from your kid. I held back most of my frustration until I'd left the room, but it was still clear to him that his words upset me, which was confusing for him.

GUT-PUNCHES

Clearly, I attached far more meaning to my son's words than what he naively intended. My reaction to his words needed some recalibrating. Owning our pride and less-than-godly moments is an extremely vulnerable self-evaluation that often starts with these sorts of gut punches. I'm convinced it's because we care about this job so much. We love being "Mom." Any performance review less than perfect feels like a fail. What if we get fired from our dream job after thinking we were nailing it? After all the tears, we always come out better though. The process of facing our shortcomings can be incredibly intimidating, but that is where the growth happens.

I am an extrovert, woman, and mother, which is basically the trifecta of what it means to be a talker. I use my fair share of words in the day, often needing to apologize later for oversharing and word vomiting on people who lend a listening ear. What I've learned along the way is that our words affect our children most of all. They are our most frequent listeners. They are around us daily, and you better believe they are observing and absorbing the way we communicate both with them and others.

That's where I found myself. Overwhelmed. I knew the way I spoke to my kids was important. I recognized I had a great influence and responsibility. I acknowledged that I needed to address my kiddos in the way they needed, not just the way that was most comfortable to me. I just didn't have it in me to actually do it. How do I motivate myself to do it?

REDECORATING

My newest favorite animal is the bumblebee. Okay, you over-achievers, I know it's technically an insect. Just go with it!

We recently built a home, and I began decorating my kitchen with yellow accents. I love yellow! Bumblebees, being both yellow and my new favorite, made the perfect touch. Bumblebees have kind of been a fad lately, so I was seeing décor with them everywhere, and I started picking some things up.

One shopping day, I saw an adorable book all about bees. Before I put it on display, I opened the book to take a peek. I mean, I've always heard "save the bees," but learning how significant these amazing little creatures were was just mind-blowing. One of the chapters was about the honey-making process (it's incredible).

God used bees as a way to get my attention in the Bible too. Now, I've read the proverbs many times before. Someone taught me there are thirty-one chapters in Proverbs and recommended I read one each day of the month. I have completed this process many times throughout my life. During one such Proverbs month, with my new love of bumblebees and their liquid gold, this verse flew off the page and landed gently on my heart.

Gracious words are a honeycomb,
sweet to the soul and healing to the bones.
Proverbs 16:24

I had just been writing out and defining the three "heart overflows" prior to reading this verse. It was one of those spiritual moments that come out of nowhere and give you goosebumps. Just a quick refresher, the three heart overflows are: the Empathetic Encourager, Back-Seat Conversationalist, and Grace-Giving Realist. The parallels I noticed in this verse are all too perfect. God stepped down and pointed my heart to see how these three communication pillars were exactly what my children needed, particularly when I struggled to regulate my own emotion or internal struggle. They were exactly what He commands us to do, but through this very unlikely verse.

THE HONEYCOMB

Look closely at the words: "*Gracious words are a honeycomb, sweet to the soul.*"

Honeybees create honeycomb cells in their hives to store their honey. Perhaps we all knew this, but I'm going to say it anyway because there's something obvious in there that I love. The honeycomb is what holds the honey. It's the crucial foundational element within a bee hive to store what they work so hard to create. The honeycomb in Proverbs 16:24 is made not of beeswax but of gracious words.

The gracious words that are *sweetness to the soul* set the foundation for our kids, our creation. And those tender and joyful words come from the heart of a Back-Seat Conversationalist. It's a selfless act to take the back seat, letting your child lead the conversation with what is important to them. It's the generous, Christ-like active listener who asks follow-up questions, stays engaged, and truly participates in the back-and-forth communication we talked about.

That is not of this world. Our world is fast-paced. Our world is achievement and results-based. Our world doesn't stop to engage with the insignificant. Yet, gracious words rest in this space. The Back-Seat Conversationalist sees value in these moments. Gracious words are not self-seeking; they forfeit their right to drive. That kind of communication with our children is *sweet.* It's something they may only ever find in their *mama.* Sweetness is something that is enjoyable. It's craved.

When your child needs to be heard, they will *crave* that time with you the way they crave and enjoy the sweetness of honey.

No time with our kids is wasted. Every moment together, we are learning to grow, even in unseen ways. Edward C. Tolman was the psychologist who first discovered and began studying this form of learning called cognitive mapping.[5] Psychologists

When your child needs to be heard, they will

crave that time with you the way they crave

and enjoy the sweetness of honey.

have piggy-backed on his work, and we now refer to it often times as latent learning. The gist is that we learn things without realizing it. We only recognize we've learned something after a situation prompts us to remember it. We don't realize in the moment we are learning, but when we look back on our past, we are then able to see how far we've come.

We put in the *hard work* of motherhood, but the enemy (and the eternal replenishment of dirty dishes and laundry) make us feel like there aren't any results—certainly none we can see! I will make a change and then look for the results immediately. I want to know that what I'm doing is worth it and working. It's tempting to give up when you don't see those instant changes. When you become the Back-Seat Conversationalist and your children don't instantly begin opening up and talking more, it could be discouraging and tempting to quit. I believe it's worth remembering how our brains use cognitive mapping. Our children will begin coming to us more when we are the Back-Seat Conversationalist, we just might not see it right away.

HEALING EMPATHY

The verse also shares that these gracious words are "*healing to the bones.*"
Meditate on that word: *healing.*

When you are compassionate with your children, you are actually *healing their bones.* The world will break them down. Your child will most certainty come home with some emotional bruises. Words said to them will cause them to ache. Scripture tells us that when we are gracious in our communication, when we step in as the Empathetic Encourager our children need, God will work through us to heal their bones. That is incredible! It gives me chills.

Just as honey has healing properties, our words can be equally healing.[6] Remember, when we start with empathy, encouragement will organically flow. Trust the power of your empathy to soothe like honey, healing your child's emotional broken bones. When you are the Empathetic Encourager, your children will most certainty run to you for healing when needing to be lifted up.

Being the mother who provides healing in the form of encouragement will ultimately set them up to achieve the calling God has on their life and reach their greatest potential.

In psychology, we base our belief of development off Maslow's Hierarchy of Needs.[7] This system shows how humans are wired in a pattern of dependencies, and it displays the correlation between meeting needs and reaching potential. The needs scale says that you cannot move to the next step until the previous step has been met.

The staircase begins with physiological needs. We must have food, water, shelter, etc. in order to continue to thrive—the resources that meet our body's survival needs. The second stair says that we need safety. We must feel secure within our environment and the people we surround ourselves with. The third stair is "love and belonging," which affirms that we need community. The fourth step is where I feel the Empathetic Encourager heart overflow resides, and that is the need of "esteem." We all have an innate need to be respected and affirmed. It is only after being esteemed that we can move to the fifth and final stair of the staircase, which is self-actualization. This is where you can reach your true potential.

If we want to be moms who equip our children to be their very best, we need to meet their needs to set them up for that success. By being the Empathetic Encourager, we are ultimately living out the fourth stair on that staircase. We are providing them the tool to continue to run up the stairs and reach their potential. Being available, providing encouragement, and showing empathy are the groundwork of love and respect.

PACING OURSELVES

Honey is a gift God made sure we knew about pretty early in our humanity. It's actually referenced many times in the Bible, oftentimes referring to something extremely valuable and good. Just as today honey is sweet and valuable, in biblical times, it too was equally as pleasing. When we consume it today, it's often a teaspoon in our tea. Sometimes we spread it on toast. Like anything of value and so rich, we don't consume a large amount.

Now, what would happen if you sat down and ate an entire jar of honey? It would probably cause you to vomit. Your stomach was not created to hold that much sweetness at once. Would consuming the entire jar add value to its sweet and healing properties? Absolutely not. Consuming too much honey wouldn't satisfy a sweet tooth, but it would cause a stomachache. Eating honey out of proportion wouldn't cause more healing to occur; it would cause for sickness.

Honey is best enjoyed within proportion. Being a mom is pretty sweet. What we need to recognize is that motherhood works best when provided in the optimal proportions. We need to allow ourselves to be the Grace-Giving Realist. We need to know that what God is using us for is valuable. It's rich and sweet and good. There's no need to spoil our

Trust the power of your empathy to soothe

like honey, healing your child's emotional

broken bones.

children's stomachs with an excess of activities. You don't have to be "on" all of the time for them or for other moms. The value of our communication comes from just being mindful of the pillars of what our children need.

Maybe you can relate to my first summer day. You thought you were doing everything right, but the connection you have with your child had somehow gotten lost. You got caught up with all the *stuff* that you forgot your purpose. After getting out a good cry, I woke up the next morning ready to go. It was a new day.

There was a psychologist by the name of Hermann Ebbinghaus in the late 1800s who dedicated his life's work to studying memory.[8] He is famous for discovering how parts of our memory operate, and is still referenced today for the finding he coined, "the forgetting curve." He ran experiments where he provided people strings of information, and asked them to remember it. He tested them often to see how long they were capable of retaining the information before they forgot.

Interestingly enough, even when told the information was important, most forgot the information within a matter of days. He used his finds to share the conclusion that if something is valuable enough to remember, we need to do it every day. Only by doing something every day will we be able to hold onto it and put place it into our long-term memories.

I believe that we can draw on the science here and use the forgetting curve as a valuable reminder. It is what we do *every day* that is going to make a difference to our children. Just as with my day valuing my work more than my kid's experience, we are going to make mistakes along the way. What really matters is what we stick with. Our patterns of behavior are what is significant, memorable, and impressionable on our children. Generally, they are going to forget the isolated events and days, but what they will remember are patterns. They are going to remember what occurs every day.

This is encouraging to me because I can be mindful of the things that happen daily in my home. I'd be convicted beyond belief if there was something wrong occurring in my home *daily*. I would be driven to address it and do something about it. I would at least be made aware. The reality—both a joy and a pain—is that being "Mom" occurs every day. We will inevitably make mistakes. There's no value in living in the past. There's value in *learning* from the past. Days get messy. There will most certainly be days when you are not a great communicator with your kids. I love the saying, "Tomorrow is here! It's called today." If you must look back, only do it for the sake of learning so that you can look forward again.

CHAPTER FIVE

The Leading Quartet

You realize how valuable defining your terms is when you ask your hubby to come home with drumsticks and he brings you chicken. I mean, every woman reading this understands I meant ice cream, right? Bring home the sweets!

These little mix-ups over what words mean in our brains is inevitable. With kids, it's sometimes a cute thing. For instance, when we play the board game *LIFE* with my son, he assumes every person's wife is named "Mary" because whenever he gets to put a pink tab in his car, we tell him he got "married." I just don't have it in me to correct him on that one. It's just way too darn cute!

But plenty of sitcoms and rom-coms can demonstrate the catastrophe of misunderstanding too. What we say and how we say it might not make sense to someone else, and without the right communication tools, it can break down relationships. This is especially the case when it comes to discussing difficult topics with our kids. The ones that we all desperately want to avoid or maybe outsource to a professional but we know we have to face.

When I arrive at this passage in 2 Timothy, I see a commandment on how us moms should be using Scripture to communicate.

All Scripture is breathed out by God and profitable for teaching, for reproof, for correction, and for training in righteousness, that the man of God may be complete, equipped for every good work.

2 TIMOTHY 3:16-17

We have to guide these little humans to be big responsible humans, and if I could have a blueprint on how to do that well, I'm all ears. Practically speaking, there are many times I value teaching my children what God's Word says, but I don't always know how to communicate it in a way that is meaningful and impactful to their lives. I'll be honest, Paul's letter here was a real head-scratcher for a while. I thought maybe he was just using four synonyms to drive home one solid point (teaching, reproof, correction, and training).

I was on board for my children being equipped—that's for sure! Equipping our children to be everything the Lord calls them to be is going to involve having wise conversations with our kids. After doing some digging, I saw these are actually four separate concepts that we can focus on to prepare for these conversations. If we could incorporate all four of these components into our conversations with our children, we could have the recipe for teaching godly living down pat, our leading quartet!

THE QUARTET

I should back up and say we shouldn't be that surprised Paul speaks on the components of *good* communication to Timothy. I can't help but think that Paul knew Timothy could relate. You see, Timothy had a grandmother and mother who left a lasting imprint on his life. Their names were Lois and Eunice, and while we don't know much about them, we are confident that their legacy of loving the Lord was passed on through Timothy because of their obedience and gift to guide him well.

> *"I am reminded of your sincere faith, a faith that dwelt first in your grandmother*
> *Lois and your mother Eunice and now, I am sure, dwells in you as well."*
> 2 TIMOTHY 1:5

I daydream on this verse. I think it would be the highest honor to be recognized as a mother or grandmother who guided my kids and grandkids well. No other credit would mean as much to me as being known for passing on the love of the Lord to my children. So, when we look back at what Paul has to share with Timothy on how to use Scripture to instruct and guide our children to live a godly life, I think we all should grab a pen and jot some of this advice down.

He begins by commanding that we need to teach. In this context, it's in relation to Scripture. Paul is not referring to tying shoes or riding a bike here. What he's talking

No other credit would mean as
much to me as being known for
passing on the love of the Lord
to my children.

about specifically is the need to instruct our kids to know what God says. We are called to teach them the Bible. It's a big, complicated book! Our children need to have an intellectual understanding of what is in God's book of communication to us. Our children will ultimately not be able to do something that they do not first know.

Memorizing verses, learning songs, and making art projects may all seem fun, but it is also impactful. We can get creative on how we teach them what God's Word says. It can totally be drawing pictures with shaving cream or saying a verse while running through a sprinkler in the backyard. Paul establishes our responsibility to introduce God's words to them, especially before we can ever expect them to act upon it.

We are then called to reproof, which is a more archaic word synonymous with "recognize." When we are reproofing our children, we are calling them to recognize the truth. Another "R" word that I use to associate with this concept is "rebuke." Ultimately, when we are recognizing the truth that we fell short of, a rebuke is needed. This is where we can instruct our children to repent (hey—there's another R word). When we first teach the truth, we can then reproof, recognize, rebuke, and repent. *Try saying that five times fast.*

Reproof is not fun for anyone involved. It's a big word, but practically speaking, we are calling our children out on the sin we see and guiding them through the process of saying "I'm sorry."

After they repent, we can move to the correction part of the verse. This is the process of setting something straight or making it right. This is where we experience restoration and our actions initiate change. This is the part where we point our children back toward godly living.

Lastly, we are called to train our children in righteousness. We can think of teaching as the "knowing" where training in righteousness is the "doing." This is the proactive moral and spiritual guidance going on within your time with your children. I believe Deuteronomy shares this type of communication and action of training in righteousness in Chapter 6:

> *"And these words that I command you today shall be on your heart. You shall teach them diligently to your children, and shall talk of them when you sit in your house, and when you walk by the way, and when you lie down, and when you rise. You shall bind them as a sign on your hand, and they shall be as frontlets between your eyes. You shall write them on the doorposts of your house and on your gates."*
>
> **Deuteronomy 6:6-9**

God's Word tells us what is true, and our job is to help our kids understand that consistently, in ways they understand, and in many different contexts. We teach and train proactively, but we are also called to communicate through reproof and correction as needed.

Paul's "Quartet" breaks down the job description of our words. Mothers are role models for their children, like Timothy's grandmother and mother were to him. We have to ensure that all four members of this quartet— teaching, reproof, correction, and training—are instruments in our ensemble.

Make no mistake. Paul was not saying the same thing four times in different words just to hear himself speak. He was specific and intentional. If we are ever going to raise the next Timothy, let's be sure we are doing all four of these with our children, and doing them well.

PREPERATION IS KEY

I like to encourage moms to ask themselves a question before ever entering into a serious talk with their kids:

Am I prepared for this conversation?

There's a lot of preparation that should go into communication. As "Mom," we do it all day long. However, we should never become desensitized to its value. it's a big deal. You are shaping another's life decisions.

When a situation calls for harder conversations such as reproof or correction, I'd like to first encourage you to scan through the environment. I want you to ask yourself, "Is this the right moment?" In other words, is it the right time and place? When we bring up a topic that we need to digest together, there should be adequate time for it (e.g., don't bring up something you found in their dresser right before baseball practice).

To ensure this is a conversation and not just "*Mom Tells Child What To Do*," we need to prepare the environment. We need to make sure we are not in line at the drive-through, getting ready for school, or headed out the door for practice. Allow your child the literal and metaphorical space to process by valuing their feelings and schedule. It helps them to recognize that this is meaningful for you, and it's not just another task on your to-do list.

We also have to make sure this is a safe place for them. Is this a spot where we can speak freely, use people's names, talk *actual events,* and be comfortable to do so? That means that nobody is around, we are in private, and that it's quiet and distraction free. They shouldn't have to speak in code, referring to "when that thing happened" with "you know who."

When you prepare your environment, you are setting the stage for communication to occur. Oftentimes, when the subject is treated as a "while I think of it," willy-nilly moment, your child "tunes out" and assumes it is either a lecture or a command, not an invitation. We get frustrated that our children are not listening or are not talking to us, but it's really a problem of environment. The environment isn't communicating the importance of the connection. So, the most important place to start is the setting. Take a look around, actually plan it out, put thought behind it, and have the environment communicate that this conversation is important, and that you are ready to connect.

After the environment is prepared, I want you to ask yourself again if you are truly prepared for this conversation.

Do you have all the facts you need to provide solid guidance? I believe this part is actually three-fold.

First, I'd start by being honest if you truly know what the Bible says about that topic. Do you know a *verse,* or do you know the passage, context, and other references that support it?

Now, those are some tall orders. I understand that not everyone, myself included, can say they know God's Word *that* well. Yet, when there is a topic that is warranting guidance-giving, I believe that a little preparation is in order. Taking time to learn what God says about it is a solid place to start.

Next, I would recommend that you do some digging to see what the research has to say. There are some amazing blogs, books, and resources out there that provide insight into many topics. This is what drove me to begin a blog. I wanted to put research into other moms' hands! We do not need to know everything. On the other side of the coin, we shouldn't give advice on something that we are not confident in ourselves. Everything I learned in psychology started with me realizing I didn't know something. Nobody was born knowledgeable. Goodness, there's plenty more I don't know than what I do. Start one conversation at a time and look up good solid support before speaking into it.

If you don't know where to start, I'd recommend asking a trusted friend. God has given us community for a reason. Chances are, a good friend has walked a similar road before you. She would be happy to share her own experience and resources with you to review. We were never meant to do this alone.

I'd end your preparation ensuring that you have all the facts right from your child's specific situation. I know I'm super guilty of this! What happens is we hear a snippet of something that went wrong, something they are struggling with, or an event that occurred—and our emotions take over. In response, we kind of blur the details. We typically heard one part that was so concerning, we almost block the rest of the story out. It happens to the best of us.

Elizabeth Loftus in the 1970s was accredited to proving the theory that our recollections and memories cannot always be trusted. I remember watching a prank show where they had someone commit a petty crime in front of a group of people. Then they waited just fifteen minutes and interviewed different members of the crowd. It was all for comedic value because they all were insisting on things that were false.[9]

Before having that wisdom-filled conversation—you know, that one you really want to avoid but still have to have—get ready. Preparation is not the same as avoidance. You are not avoiding or procrastinating; you simply want to do the conversation justice, and there is some real value in that. You may have the right moment, but are lacking the content prep. Or maybe you dedicated lots of time to craft your message, but you are struggling to find the opportunity. Maybe you are not quite sure you can say with certainty what needs to be addressed based on your recollection of the incident. There will absolutely be some time-specific conversations that have to be had, but so many could benefit from hitting the pause button to ensure they are inviting a fruitful conversation.

It makes me think of how I choose and evaluate restaurants and meals now. I love me a good meal. As I get older, I appreciate food all the more (probably because I cook a lot of it). When I go out to eat, I enjoy evaluating the flavors and pretending I actually know what I'm talking about. I'm also easily fooled by appearance. If I'm in a nice restaurant, and the presentation of the meal is beautifully arranged, or the place is nicely decorated, the food magically seems to taste better. The food didn't change, but the preparation for me to enjoy was enhanced.

We might think we'd say the same thing—"serve the same meal"—whether it's at our sticky, plain kitchen counter with kids, dogs, and husbands scurrying around or at a mahogany table with fine china, a gorgeous chandelier, and beautiful music. But when we pay attention to the preparation and environment of the significant conversations we have with our kids, we're both able to gain more and enjoy more from the experience.

Life is busy. We can't have fine china and toddlers—I get that. There's not many opportunities for preparation as much as glimpses of "word vomiting" and lecturing.

When we can, and when the topic is not time sensitive, let's not be so quick to discount the value of adding some frill to the meal.

CONVERSING WELL

Research helps us in the teaching and conversation process. There have been so many findings on how to communicate in a way that allows our children to understand. One thing that is clear in the literature is that questions are your friend. We do not and should not be doing all the talking. When we do all the talking, it's no longer a conversation.

When a group of teenagers were polled on their parents' conversations, this was their number-one complaint. They didn't mind that their parents gave them guidance and talked about the hard stuff. Goodness, they actually kind of wanted it. What they didn't like, though, was when it became a speech.[10] A good way for us to avoid this is to ask more questions!

When we ask questions, we not only avoid speech-giving and invite conversation, but we drive the content. In my experience, most difficult conversations do not play out the way that I imagined they would. They often take twists and turns. Within the midst of the conversation, I learn about a struggle they've been having, I learn something new about their opinions and values, or I walk away seeing that I misread the situation altogether.

Questions help guide the content so you know exactly what to focus on rather than sharing a bunch of one-liners and pre-scripted phrases on something that might actually be irrelevant. Something we'd all realize to be true if we asked more and talked less.

Another amazing value of asking questions is that it allows for us to know exactly *how much* we should share. The way that our children respond will indicate where the answer needs to go. It will allow for us to gain insight on what is needed within the moment. There are so many topics where a wise conversation with our children is needed, but often those topics run deep. Let me name a few to get your ideas flowing: racism, puberty, cyberbullying, purity, politics, war, etc. You may think these are too extreme or advanced for your child, but I guarantee the time is coming...probably sooner than you can think.

For example, my son recently completed his first ALICE drill at school. For those of you not familiar, that is the drill where students learn how to respond if an active shooter were to enter into their school. I have to say, the school did a great job of providing the parents handouts and educational materials on exactly what they were teaching

Questions help guide the content so you know exactly what to focus on rather than sharing a bunch of one-liners and pre-scripted phrases on something that might actually be irrelevant.

the students. They did this with the hope that the parents would continue to talk and process the drill with them once they returned home.

I knew this drill was needed, but deep down, it really made me sick to my stomach. I was nervous and fretting on how my innocent son would process the big, dark, evil concept of a dangerous person entering his school with the intent to harm him. During dinner, I asked him about how his drill went and if he had any questions. The only thing I got from him was that his special spot was by the computer and that it was super important that he be quiet and listen to his teacher if he heard that alarm go off.

I responded with, "How do you feel about that?"

He went on to tell me how excited he was that his spot was by the computer because he really wanted that spot!

It absolutely makes me chuckle now, but I was really prepared to have a "why are there bad people in this world" talk with him. I was totally ready to go into guidance mode and talk all about how we should be prepared but not scared. Yet in his little mind, he was just thrilled to be placed by the computer.

This is why it's *so important* to ask questions prior to diving in to guidance. By asking how he felt, I was able to assess that there was no need to have a deep talk with him that night. Consequently, if I would have divulged that information without asking questions when his heart wasn't ready, it most certainly would have caused more harm than good. Or maybe it would have just gone way over his head!

Another thing to consider when having wise conversations is their individuality. It is tempting to just speak out of the abundance of who you are and what you've learned. We need to be honest with ourselves if we want to be wise mamas.

Are you telling them everything that *you would do,* or are you allowing for individuality and choice? As therapeutic as we might find it, we are not raising ourselves. If you have multiple children, you are not raising the same person times two, three, or four. They are all special individuals with brains that function in unique order that may or may not have commonalities with others. Allowing them to feel valued despite making different choices than you or their siblings makes a lasting impact on their development. It shows that you love and respect them as an individual. We are still absolutely there to teach them the right way, but let's make sure we are not just allowing *our* way. Our way is ultimately a preference, where the right way, God's way, should be the only non-negotiable.

If your child isn't going against something that is clearly said to be wrong in Scripture, but rather it's just not the way *you would do it,* why not entertain that? They may choose a way that's longer, harder, and inefficient. *Eh, why not?* Let them try. Verbal explanation can only go so far. As some point, and with some personality types, experience is everything. They need to experience it for themselves in order to learn. Trust me, you'll want them to experience the consequences of their choices when they are young—when things are simpler. The more you hold on, the more they will sometimes pull. There comes a point where experience needs to be the guidance.

WALK THE TALK

One of the most beneficial things you can do when preparing those hard conversations where solid guidance is required is to ensure you take the guidance yourself. Our children are the most amazing detectives. They can spot hypocrisy a mile away! They know when you are walking the walk versus just talking the talk. Live out the guidance you give. They will sniff it out and call your bluff. Even if they are too young to truly notice, they will notice as they age, and it will be a mess of mistrust.

I often get the question: "What if I don't want my child to do something, but I myself have done it?" In that scenario, I'd say you must own it. That is the best way to do it. You have to be honest with them on a time something didn't work out well for you. Maybe tell your story and why it means so much that they do not do it themselves. However, if it can be restituted in any regard, it's also equally important that you try to remedy the situation.

For example, if you advise them that you do not want them to smoke, but you still smoke, it is okay to tell them not to smoke. Share your story and why you regret your decision. However, you should also be taking steps to quit smoking. That will yield the sincerest guidance.

There are other things that continually occur despite your best effort. For example, yelling when angry.

If you give guidance why you shouldn't yell when angry, but then you engage in that action, an apology is in order. Recognize that you made a mistake, ask for forgiveness, and share how you will try not to do that again in the future: "I'm sorry Mommy yelled at you. I was angry. Do you forgive me? Next time I'll count to ten because yelling when angry is not appropriate."

When we mess up in a specific way we've advised they not, sharing exactly how you plan to refrain in the future is admirable.

Are you still with me?

I think we all could use a deep breath.

INFLUENCE, NOT CONTROL

We have been given the assignment of training our children in the way they should go. That is our job description per the Lord. Nowhere in that job description does it tell us that we are to control them, though. Nowhere does it tell us we should force them to do it the right way. We can't control or force anyone to comply. Ultimately, forced compliance is not compliance at all. That is also why God's Word assures us that we are not responsible for the outcome. We all would love the outcome to be, "and then they listened to my guidance and we all lived happily ever after." Ha, wouldn't that be nice? Unfortunately, that is not always how it works.

God's Word shares with us time and time again that we are to focus on our part. We are not called to control but to influence. Cue the quartet! That is where these conversations appear—as we are playing our quartet, ensuring all four commanded parts of communication make an appearance in the way we speak and engage with our children.

After you act as their example—teach, reproof, correct, and train—it's your child's job to wrestle with the Lord and digest the truth you are sharing with them. Our part is to guide. Our part is to lead.

We just cannot focus on controlling the outcome. We can most certainly pray for them, and from there, we can rest in knowing that we are not in charge of the end result. God is sovereign and will work that part out. We can trust Him for that.

The passage in 2 Timothy 3 says that when we do our part, our child will be equipped for every good work. It doesn't give us the guarantee that they will do the good that we have modeled for them, but they most certainty will have the tools in their toolbox. There is great hope that they will pull them out one day.

Not everyone will play in the game, but by equipping them, you are giving them the uniform shall they ever want to be on the roster one day.

Maybe your child is in the phase where they do not ask for your consult. Or maybe you are blessed to have a tender-hearted child that truly does welcome your insight. When they come to you with a problem, it's likely that your recommendations will include things such as: saying no, leaving a sticky situation, working hard, talking through the difficult thing, or a plethora of other things that are not necessarily pleasant. They did, after all, come to you because there was a *problem.* You are providing that advice within your guidance because you know that is what is best, but you know it will not fall on eager ears when you share! As a result, sometimes our well-meaning selves overcompensate for our kids.

We want to help, so after they come to us for guidance on a particular topic, we lovingly jump in with both feet! We are so thrilled they want our insight that we then begin to overstep. If we are not careful, we can begin to do things for them, remove responsibilities, or orchestrate events to go in their favor. We falsely think they trusted us with this concern or problem, so if we don't "solve it," they won't come to us again.

However, we must not confuse them coming to us for guidance as our responsibility to fix the issue they needed guidance on. It's still their responsibility, their choice, their problem to solve. We shouldn't be doing it for them. Rather, we should be guiding *them* on how to do it. If you step in and meddle, that will be extremely confusing for the child. They will never learn what guidance is. We will blur the lines of guidance and enabling.

As their moms, we are called to provide them the knowledge they need through teaching, reproof, correction, and training in righteousness. This is the symphony for wise conversations that Paul writes for us to follow. These wise conversations ultimately end with an action step for the child, not for you. We should probably do something after the conversation too. We could pray, follow up, and be more observant in the area we spoke on. The action to respond, though, is up to the child. Taking away that step for them will cripple the process.

The hard lessons are only learned through experience sometimes. To some degree, your child needs to experience it. It's a skill that needs to be built. Experience builds character. When we take those opportunities away from them by overstepping and meddling, we are doing them such a disservice. We are taking away their opportunity for growth.

Let me say it again, mama. You are *not* responsible for the outcome. You are only responsible for your words and actions. Use your judgment, set boundaries, implement consequences, provide good guidance, and keep playing the instruments. At the end of the day, that is something to be proud of, regardless of how the problem may play out, because you'll know they are equipped.

CHAPTER SIX

The Guidance Guide

received a phone call from the school. The woman on the other end of the phone was the principal. My heart sank. My first thought was *principals do not call parents.*

I first asked, "Is he okay?"

I was hoping for reassurance, but instead what I received was, "Well, there's been an incident on the playground." At that point, I felt like I left fingerprints in my phone because I was squeezing it so tightly. Thankfully, she went on to share that he wasn't seriously hurt. However, a kid on the playground had punched him in the eye.

You see, he is my little leader. Apparently, there was another child acting like a bully on the playground during recess that day. He claimed a section of the playground equipment to himself and wasn't letting any other friends play. The other students decided it wasn't worth the conflict, and they walked away. My son? Oh no, he needed to make a point. He walked right up to a kid twice his size and told him, "You are not being very nice, and you need to share with my friends." Consequently, he walked away with a black eye.

I prepared my speech for when he came home. This was a defining moment in motherhood. God has great wisdom and guidance about leadership, forgiveness, courage—my boy needed to hear my heartfelt, thoroughly planned guidance on the situation that was in no way influenced by the fact that he was my baby who had a black eye. When he came home that day, I embodied the Empathetic Encourager and said,

Drumroll, please…

"Stay away from that boy!"

85

Not a perfect empathetic encouragement.

I really did say that, though. I wanted him to really understand, so I even quizzed him a few times that night.

I would say things like, "So if he comes by you again at recess, what are you going to do?"

He would answer, "I'm going to stay away from him, Mama."

I would respond, "Yes, stay away from him. He's not nice."

When picking him up from school the next day, I was wide-eyed wondering how his day had gone. He couldn't get into the car quick enough!

"So," I asked, drawing out the Os. "How did your day go? Did that boy leave you alone today?"

He was all smiles. He responded, "No, Mom. He is actually really nice now. We decided to be friends."

"Friends?!"

But we went through the plan!

We very clearly decided that we were staying far, far away from this child. Now, he was going to be *friends* with Mr. Punches? Um, hard no!

Okay, time to try giving some empathetic, encouraging guidance.

"No. We are not going to be friends with him. He is not nice, and we are not friends with people who punch people."

THINK WIDER

As mothers, we are our kids' compasses for two decades—arguably longer according to some! We are not involved just in the small or large experiences. We *are* their experience. We are there, or we relive it with them, and our purpose is to guide and teach their little minds how to process and respond to these events in healthy ways. We are called to give them *guidance*. Guidance, however, is quite a tricky thing.

We are called to guide and advise our children who, despite their youth, think they know best or are stubbornly immature. They operate and decide with an underdeveloped brain and a limited perspective, so they really just want their way. Nobody likes to be corrected and told which way to go. I mean, if we are honest, that is how we are at times too.

We all want to navigate the world in the way we feel is best. When we combine our desire for control with the overwhelming pressure to make sure our children *turn out right*, we find quite the predicament. Usually, it involves Mom demanding her way while her child does everything *but* that way. It's a classic power struggle where Mom says "black" and child says "white." There's defeat, hopelessness, and chaos. When they don't listen to our guidance, we're tempted to throw our arms up in defeat.

A common guidance "trap" that I notice a lot—and have been plenty guilty of myself—is narrow-mindedness. We look at the circumstance too specifically and lose the generality of what the advice should include. When we zoom in too close at a particular situation, we are quickly entangled in the small details. We will quickly rationalize exceptions and thus overcomplicate the scenario. We can get so caught in the details of what happened that we lose sight of the problem and why we were called in to help.

Our guidance should be generalizable. This means that our children can apply it and discern within future scenarios even if we're not there. This makes sense, right? The chances of them encountering the exact same scenario are very slim. The chances of them encountering a similar situation is pretty likely. When we narrow our focus and guidance to a specific scenario, we lose the opportunity to teach wisdom, understanding, and the general principles behind making a decision.

TRY IT

If our child gets into a tug-a-war match over a toy, we could talk about sharing rather than the circumstance. If our child calls another a bad name, we could talk about appropriate problem-solving rather than using not bad words. Focus on what we *want them to do* moving forward. We also need to find the teachable moment within the circumstance that can be generalized (e.g., sharing, problem solving, etc.) rather than getting down to their "he said/she did" detective work.

Mamas, try to find phrases and verses to continually come back to and repeat when parenting in this way. When we use the same phrase and verse multiple times to explain a concept, the chances are much higher of them associating the situation with that verse or phrase, "getting it," and generalizing it to other circumstances.

The psychologist David McClelland determined that there were three main motivators in life for everyone.[11] There is the need to influence others and gain status, which is the driving motivation for power. There is the driving motivator of achievement, which

When we narrow our focus and guidance

to a specific scenario, we lose the

opportunity to teach wisdom,

understanding, and the general principles

behind making a decision.

is the need to set and meet goals. Lastly, we all have the driving motivation of affiliation, which is the need to work alongside others and collaborate. Typically, when one of these motivators are challenged, a conflict will ensue.

Hence, it makes sense that when someone knocks down a tower a child built, they may begin to cry. Their driving motivator for achievement was rocked. It's useful to think in these terms at times because we realize our brains work in generalities as well. We become upset in specific and individual circumstances because of the wider patterns of human nature. By providing advice that is generalizable, we are equipping them on how to respond the next time their driving motivator is challenged in a different way.

STABILIZE YOUR EMOTIONS

In addition to generalizable advice, we also have to caution ourselves not to provide emotionally blinded advice. Emotionally blind advice occurs when we become so emotionally involved in a situation, we make decisions that don't seem rational to the outside person. It usually occurs when we engage in a phenomenon called *Emotional Reasoning,* which is when we convince ourselves that our feelings are fact.[12]

One example of this happened in my office. A mother had a tense relationship with her daughter's school. Many conflicts had eroded her trust in the personnel. When she did not receive paperwork from the school that she needed, she burst into tears of frustration and exasperation. These strong emotions blinded her guidance to her daughter. She shared with her child the need to challenge authority at the school because she did not trust them to have her daughter's best interest at heart. Even though her daughter did not have these experiences, she began to fear school, struggled with anxiety, and refused to go because she no longer felt safe. Unintentionally, her mother had allowed her own feelings to cloud her judgment and instruction for her child. What she said was based on her own circumstances and emotions, not what her child needed. This mom saw the effects of her actions, and she was left with regret that she acted on her emotions. It was true that the school was dropping the ball and disappointing her, but her daughter sadly paid the price in a much more significant and unnecessary way.

She's certainly not alone. Our emotions are powerful! They pull us like a puppy on a leash, and without the right training and education, they can lead us down dark paths.

I become emotionally charged when I am stressed, and nothing stresses me out more than having to give guidance on a big issue. I freeze. I feel the weight of the moment and think that I'm going to get it wrong. I'm going to say the wrong thing, give the wrong consult, and they will remember the conversation forever. I have nightmares that as an adult, my boys will start a sentence with: "Remember the time I came to you upset, and you told me…"

Believing I'm completely right is also a recipe for emotional blindness. When I see something that needs to be addressed and want to tackle it head-on, my emotions are raging. The warning light here is when we believe we are one hundred percent *right* and the other person is one hundred percent *wrong*. This is rarely the case in life. You can count the number of times you will know everything or are absolutely morally perfect while the other person knows nothing or is objectively wrong on one hand.

To avoid giving that emotionally blinded advice, I recommend putting some time and space between you and the situation before you talk to your child. If you are like me, you may feel this intense need to address the situation immediately. That is another abundance of misplaced emotion. There is no harm is waiting, cooling off, and getting more facts and potential solutions before to sharing advice. The last thing we want to do is to *change* our advice, especially if it ends up being too late. If we share guidance on how to do something, we need to ensure it generalizable and unchanging. The way we can assure that occurs is by waiting until you are ready to talk.

This very concept was studied by psychologists Daniel Kahneman and Amos Tversky in the 1990s. They developed a new theory to explain how we make decisions. They proposed that there are two different ways we arrive at a conclusion: System 1 and System 2. In essence, System 1 refers to the decisions we make quickly.[13] These are highly reactive and require little conscious thought. The opposite, then, is System 2, which refers to decisions we make after consideration, factual evidence, and time. I don't believe it's shocking that they determined System 1 quick decision-making led to more unjustified conclusions. Quick decision-making can be valuable, but is often based upon biased thinking patterns. System 2's slow decision-making considers the implications of a situation before responding.

The difference between emotionally biased guidance and well-thought guidance is primarily time. If we can slow down, time itself will lead to better guidance.

THE *NEXT-TIME* CONVERSATION

One of the ways we must guide is through discipline. Our children misbehaved, but we can use this as a guiding and teachable moment. Sure, there are consequences. Some are natural consequences such as getting hurt because they were running inside or losing their change because they didn't put it in their pocket when you asked. They made a choice and the consequence was decided for them. The other kind of consequence is the one we give. These can be described as punishment. We either add something as a result of their behavior, such as a time-out or extra chores, or we take something away, like TV privileges or special snacks.

Regardless of whether the consequence for their action was a natural one or something that you determined, I'd always recommend having a conversation about what occurred with your child after the misbehavior and discipline (consequence). This is when we provide the guidance they need to prevent a "next time." This guidance is the tie-together, why-it's-worth-the-hard-work kind of part.

During the "next-time conversation," allow your child to be the talker. Remember, as mom, we usually do too much talking already. Now it's their turn. You are the listener. This conversation may occur a day or week after the incident, but I recommend before they go to bed the day it occurred. I personally find this to be the "sweet spot" where it is still fresh in their minds but they are also calmed down and emotionally removed some. Them being a tad emotionally removed will allow them to accept the guidance, similar to why we too need time to ensure we are not emotionally blinded.

This conversation can go a little bit like this:

Mom: Hey Max, do you remember when I asked you to pick up today and you yelled at me?

Max: Yes, Mama. I'm sorry.

Mom: What do you think you could do *next time?*

One of four (ish) responses may occur. They may be able to tell you a better way.

I should have asked for more time.

I could have picked up my blocks so that we could leave.

I should have made a game out of it.

The opposite could be true, too. They could say the famous, "I don't know."
It's in this part of the conversation that you can incorporate a teachable moment and

provide some other solutions if it happened again. Share some appropriate ways they could meet that need in the future.

You may find that coming up with appropriate way to meet that desire or need are actually kind of difficult. It allows us to be a bit more understanding that making the right choice may be harder than it looks. Or maybe you see how they didn't see any other way. They truly didn't know the "right" way to act in that circumstance. By chance, maybe you didn't see the full picture. Maybe there was something going on that you didn't realize?

After you process the misbehavior together and suggest how to work through it next time, offer *forgiveness* and *grace*. If they apologize, you forgive. You then follow it up with grace by using relatability. I'd encourage you to share: "I try to be the best Mom I can be but sometimes I make mistakes, too."

Share something you wish you didn't do that day. Ask for *their* forgiveness. Show them that you are not perfect either. You are there to correct and be their authority, but you can sympathize with them.

JESUS' EXAMPLE

I imagine God wanting to have these talks with me every day too—desiring for me to confess my own mistakes, take ownership of them, and ask for His forgiveness (which He readily gives). If and when I make time for these kinds of conversations, God is eager to help me learn, grow, and live without so many painful consequences in life. The crazy thing is, He was in my shoes, so everything He says comes from a profound place of empathy and understanding that I may not have trusted if I didn't know the story of Jesus.

The idea that Jesus came to earth has more implications that I can ever fathom. I cannot wrap my mind around the perfection of His plan of redemption, but that's okay. I'm content knowing I can't understand all of His ways. Jesus was one-hundred-percent God and yet one-hundred-percent man while on this earth. He never compromised being God, but He selflessly created a way for us to know and love Him deeper, even when it cost Him greatly.

"For we do not have a high priest who is unable to sympathize with our weaknesses, but one who in every respect has been tempted as we are, yet without sin. Let us then with confidence draw near to the throne of grace."

HEBREWS 4:15-16

His cost for being human was not only the crucifixion, but all of the ugly things He never needed to endure before. He felt all our temptations, yet He remained God, flawless and perfect. He experienced physical fatigue, hunger, thirst, stomachaches, annoying politicians, and sweaty summers. Jesus was born like all of us were, lived and breathed the way we do, and did not ever step away from the Father. This was always His intricate plan. To know us on a relational level, to feel the temptation of sin, yet to choose not to engage it in so that He could go on to save us from our helpless state.

This greatly impacts the way that I mother. *He gets us.* He endured the human condition and overcame it so He could counsel us through it too. Being relatable to our children and showing them that we too become tempted with sin allows our children to draw near to us with a sense of safety and vulnerability. As a family, we're in humanity together with God as our true leader.

We are allowed the opportunity to be the reflective mirror of the Lord. We can be relatable and approachable, ready to forgive while also modeling sound truth, which is what we will use to steer what we say.

DISCONNECTING TO BE CONNECTED

Because we are emotional beings, we sometimes emotionally set boundaries and disconnect. If we do not personally experience feelings about something, it must mean we don't care!

Don't worry. That's not the truth.

There are actually times we need to disconnect ourselves emotionally in order to best serve. This is especially true in the area of counseling our kids.

We need to put our logical hats on and think through things clearly and rationally. We are about to give guidance that will shape the way they view the world around them, and alter the way they respond. That is a big deal, so we need to double-check that we are not allowing our emotions, biases, or anything not grounded in truth to cloud our judgment.

We can learn from the story of Rebekah and the guidance that she gave her son, Jacob. The passage says she loved and favored her son, and she allowed her emotions to play a role in the guidance that she gave him. She desperately wanted her favorite son, Jacob, to be given the blessing from her husband, his father. She then commanded Jacob to lie and cheat to get it. Her son Jacob even questioned this guidance, but she insisted upon it:

Being relatable to our children and showing them that we too become tempted with sin allows our children to draw near to us with a sense of safety and vulnerability.

"His mother said to him, 'Let your curse be on me, my son;
only obey my voice, and go, bring them to me.'"

Genesis 27:13

Rebekah had influence on Jacob. What was the outcome? Her son went on to lie and cheat, following her instruction. He deceived his brother, but it doesn't stop there. We read in Scripture how deception follows both his life and the life of his family for twenty years. Jacob became the victim of deceit by his uncle and his sons later.

This reminds me of the famous Stanley Milgram study conducted to study our response to authority figures. Stanley Milgram ran the study at Yale University in the 1960s.[14] The experiment involved participants electrically shocking other participants when an authority figure instructed them to, testing when each would reach their limit on complying with an authority figure versus obeying their conscience. The electric shocks were not real, and everyone but the person in charge of administering the shocks were actors aware of the study and its intent. Milgram's study demonstrated the impact authority has on our decision-making, even when we disagree.

Our children can easily be persuaded to act against their own conscience. It is completely normal and encouraged to want your child to prosper and experience blessings. We just have to caution ourselves not to have that desire dominate and influence our advice in sinful or deceitful ways. Removing ourselves emotionally from the subject while providing instruction is one way we can keep this bias in check. Disconnect from our own emotions, desires, and wants for our child, and connect on what the truth is.

BRINGING IT HOME

The very next day after my sweet son said he was besties with "Punches," a Wednesday after school, we were doing our weekly Bible lesson. It was the story of Zacchaeus.

"Ah," I thought. I knew this story. The little tax collector man was in the tree (he was too short to see Jesus in the crowd) and Jesus said, "Come down" and went to his house that night. Cute story, right? Well, let me tell you. I felt like I was the one sucker-punched when we got into the heart of the message that day.

You see, Zacchaeus was a bad dude. Taxes weren't exactly coded like the IRS nowadays. He cheated and robbed people of money. He was self-serving and prideful. Jesus said He wanted to eat at his house that night *before* Zacchaeus repented. Jesus was a friend to the "bad guy," and in response to Jesus' great love, Zacchaeus was forever changed.

It may sound silly to you, but—hand to my heart—literal tears filled my eyes that afternoon. I was so incredibly moved. I gave my son a huge hug and told him I was proud of him. He looked at me all strange.

"Buddy, you were like Jesus on the playground!" I beamed. "That boy was mean to you, yet you showed him love anyway. Then, he became nice after he saw your kindness."

I was so proud. He didn't fully get it, but it didn't matter. *I got it.* God used this example to teach me a great lesson that day.

The initial guidance I gave wasn't exactly careful. My emotions and protective instincts clouded the ways God could use my kind son. I also told him what to do immediately instead of taking some time to really think through it and ask for more information. We need to be really thoughtful with the guidance that we give. Now, was I wrong for telling him to stay away from that boy? Eh, it's debatable. I don't think it was *wrong*, and I'm sure there's plenty of arguments why he should have probably moved on and kept his distance. When I reflect back though, I knew my heart in that moment, and I was being too narrow-minded in the details of the event. I was emotionally blinded and it clouded my judgment. My son was actually there though, and he knew that boy just needed a friend.

We are given the opportunity to speak truth and shape another person's life. Who knows what our kids will go on to accomplish? You have the opportunity to allow that person to be everything God made them to be. That is a gift! What a privilege it is to speak truth into these young minds.

CHAPTER SEVEN

Discipline
with Purpose

We've all been in a crowded room when something crashes, or we begin to hear the screaming and bickering. We look up in terror: "Was that *my* kid?"

It's funny how quick we are to panic in humiliation when it is our own kids mildly disrupting the peace, but how little we judge anyone else's children for the same thing.

"It's okay! Don't worry about it!" we say.

We laugh and put the other mom at ease. We may even assure her, "My kid does that all the time."

As a behavior therapist, this is my specialty. I've had the privilege of helping hundreds of clients change unwanted behavior they saw in their children. Everything from tantrums, aggression, refusal, right down to potty training and getting them to eat their vegetables. There is hope for *all* behavior to change. I promise you, there is never an unhealthy behavior that cannot be shaped.

That being said, if we are going to stop unwanted behavior, we need to start discipling better. We need to discipline with a purpose. There is no *one* consequence that should be used as a response to all behavior.[15]

For example, a time-out could be used for hitting their sibling, but not effective for refusing to eat their dinner. It all comes down to why they are doing it. Why did they engage in that behavior? That is going to be the key to unlock what consequence will work best. The good news is why we do anything can be narrowed down to a few reasons.[16] Let's break down the main ones together.

ATTENTION

One reason our children (or people in general) misbehave, which usually comes as no surprise to parents, is attention. This is probably the most common reason why people do what they do. There are many different types of attention people seek. They may want positive attention (praise), or negative attention (scolding). Yes, there are times people would prefer the negative. The learned behavior a child discovers is that negative attention is easier to gain, so that is what they begin to associate attention with. The fact that it's a tad dysfunctional doesn't matter to them. They are simply solving a problem and meeting a need.

In addition to paying attention to them specifically, sometimes they prefer our attention on something that is important to them. For children, sometimes that game, craft, show, or song is what they want us to focus our attention on. They don't necessarily want our attention on them but on what they see as being important within the moment.

Public attention is another subcategory, which comes in the form of compliments and recognition. There are also times that they want a specific person's attention. They could be the center of attention, but if they are not receiving *the person's* attention that they are seeking, they still misbehave.

For younger children, the most common thing to look for is their eye contact. If they are having a true meltdown of some sort, they will generally become so dysregulated, they won't be making eye contact. They will generally be dropping to the floor, squeezing something tightly, yelling, etc. Consequently, if they are doing all of those things and still making eye contact with you, or if they keep looking back at your reaction, chances are the reason is for attention.

For older children, this morphs into your classic power struggle. This is where they try to trap you in your words. They argue, negotiate, talk back, and try to push your buttons.

If you ever feel like they are trying to get you to lose your temper, this is generally how older children present their attention-seeking behavior. At this age, they will generally want to walk away or remove themselves if upset, so if they continually stay and want to engage, I would take that as a sign they are looking for attention.

ESCAPE

The second reason I see misbehavior is to escape something that is non-preferred. This can be an expectation, chore, item on their schedule, or anything that is not desirable for them in the moment. They simply do not want to comply.

Most times, this is a task that they do not want to complete, but sometimes it may be a bit deeper than that. Maybe it is something that they actually really enjoy doing, but it's not being done their way. The idea of it not being done exactly the way it is in their mind is too much for them. You will see them try to escape the new way and see their way through.

Along the same lines, it could be something they enjoy, but it's not done at their preferred time. Maybe there was a schedule change, and the change is something they are trying to escape, so they recreate what was "supposed" to happen. Maybe it is something in their environment that they are trying to escape. They do not like a particular sound, person, or activity. This can cause them to not want to be a part of the situation any longer. Lastly, look into conversations as well. Maybe they are avoiding a conversation about something they want to escape from.

Most commonly for younger children, I see this behavior when it comes time for expectations and rules. They do not want to clean up their blocks. They do not want to set the table. They do not want to leave the birthday party. They simply do not prefer what is being asked of them, and they cope with misbehavior.

With older children, to me, they sometimes act a bit more discrete with this one. They have learned that if they make a scene, they will be disciplined. However, if they are *quietly* disobedient, this is a lot more effective. It might be continually asking for more time, saying "okay" but then never really following through, or just simply ignoring their parent's requests. All of this could be categorized as escape behavior.

TANGIBLE

Everything that you can see and touch fall into the fall into the category of behavior affected by tangible things. For example: toys, snacks, screens, and everything in between. I mention those three in particular because they tend to come up the most.

Generally, the behavior is occurring in this category because they want something. They are seeking out an item that is usually being denied. It could be denied or withheld because you told them they couldn't have it, that their time was finished, or a peer took it from them. Any circumstance where they want something, do not get it, and misbehave falls under this reason.

Outside of the three most common tangibles (toys, snacks, and screens), money is a strong motivator for older children. A tangible could also be considered an activity, such as them wanting to do a puzzle, board game, or even playing a make-believe game such as "house" or tag. Most of the tangibles that we see misbehaviors over are all considered privileges. It's something that is a privilege in life that they want more of or more time with.

Younger children typically struggle with sharing. Have you ever been on a play date and watch the excitement that comes over the visiting child's face? New toys! What tends to happen next is a back-and-forth exchange as they go from "This is so exciting!" to "Why is this person touching my things?"

SOLUTION TIME

When we uncover the reason for why children misbehave, it's only natural to hope for a solution. My whole career rests on the joy of providing these solution strategies to families. That's the beauty of finding out why they are doing something. We find out this information because there are evidence-based solutions that can bring real change!

Before we move on, I do not want to give you the false idea that this will is a one-size-fits-all type system.

> *Max is doing this for attention. I'll insert the attention solution strategy, and behavior will certainly disappear.*

That does happen sometimes, but most times it happens more like:

> *Max is doing this for attention. I'll insert the attention solution, I'll run many cycles of this solution strategy, and then after much effort, we reach a breakthrough.*

In all actuality, the behavior can get worse before it gets better. The way a child responds to the solution strategy depends on so many variables, their environment, personality, duration the behavior has been occurring, and how powerful the motivation for the behavior is. Just like there is not a one-size-fits-all behavior strategy, there is not a one-size-fits-all process to change. The hope to hold onto here is that if you are consistent, regardless of the process, behavior change will come. It takes time. If you are consistent—

ahem, let me say that again: if you are *consistent*

Just like there is not a one-size-fits-all behavior strategy, there is not a one-size-fits-all process to change.

—then with time, I can assure you the behavior will dissipate. You will have change. You are, after all, teaching them a new skill. Just like any new skill, it is going to take them time and practice to learn. They are going to naturally be resistant to it. If you implement a solution strategy and it "works" immediately, I'm immediately skeptical. Generally, if you respond and it stops the behavior on the first try, you have just given them what they wanted.

NO LONGER MEETING THAT NEED

I really do love a clear plan. I will most certainty get to the evidence-based solution strategies for each reason of behavior. If I can, I want to take you one step back though and give you a behind-the-scenes look as to why these solution strategies are effective. I know personally when I understand *why* I'm doing something, it makes it easier for me to see it through. Seeing these solutions through will not be a cake walk. This parenting takes intentionality and a streak of stubbornness. I believe knowing why will be helpful in the midst of those hard times.

When it comes to misbehavior, chances are they are meeting a need in an inappropriate way. They do need to meet that need. Most times, the need is valid. The problem is the method they are using to meet it. That is why we are disciplining and not serving. We are in corrective mode rather than assisting. If you want to highlight and star this next line, this will be your goal for discipline.

> *It's my responsibility to teach them that their misbehavior will no longer meet that need.*

That really is the whole point.

If they are talking back for attention, we are going to be sure they do not receive any attention. Talking back does not meet their need for attention any longer. If they are throwing a fit to escape a chore, then we will ensure that we see it through until the chore is completed. Throwing a fit no longer allows them to not to do their chores. If they are whining for a tangible, we will be sure they do not have access to that object.

It's my responsibility to teach them that yelling no longer allows them to have access to privileges.

If you provide them the need (attention, escape, tangible) that they are seeking after or during an inappropriate behavior, you are reinforcing their negative behavior. You are teaching them that their inappropriate behavior has power. You are showing them that being inappropriate allows them to have their needs, desires, and wants met. If what they are doing *works,* then they will just continue to do it. By *giving in,* we are showing them that misbehavior is highly effective.

Despite all our best wishes and prayers, most children are still developing the moral compass we want them to have. It's under construction. It's forming. I would say it's *in progress* to varying degrees depending on their salvation and understanding of the gospel, but overall, it's elementary at best. Expecting a child to not do something solely because it's not right is most times not enough. We need to be explaining and showing them why that behavior is not acceptable and why God doesn't want us to act in that way; following it through with no longer meeting the need. We need to show them their misbehavior is not effective. That is what will ultimately change their behavior long-term.

If we follow with our "No Longer Meeting the Need" philosophy of behavior, then when your child engages in a behavior for attention, make sure they do not receive attention during that time. Break the attention-seeking cycle. Remember that eye contact, physical touch, and other non-verbal actions are still attention.

I'd recommend starting with a sympathetic statement. You can say something like, "I can see you are really upset, and I want to help you." Go first and extend that olive branch.

You then provide your expectation afterwards. It will sound something like this: "I can help you when you have a safe body and a calm voice." You clearly state *when* you can help. That is going to be when they are no longer engaging in the bad behavior and doing something appropriate instead. Notice I didn't say, "When you stop (talking back, fighting with your brother, etc.)." That is not telling them what they should be doing. We want to focus on what *will* access your attention in that moment.

Then, you will simply wait. Do something that does not engage with them or provide them attention. Pretend to read a book, fold the laundry, continue cooking dinner, etc. You can check in (every one to ten minutes depending on the age, situation, and your preference) and see if you can help. Only say your initial phrase, "I can help you when you have a safe body and a calm voice." Continue to wait. Once they are appropriate, go ahead and jump on in, Mama!

They did it, you did it, and now you can talk through a solution.

It will not always be an attention-seeking cause. When a child is trying to escape out of a non-preferred or undesirable activity or expectation, it's going to be a rough one.

It is our responsibility to teach them that this behavior no longer meets their desire to escape. For escape specifically, when they throw a tantrum, they still need to clean up their blocks. When they pout in the corner, it's still time to go to school. You need to see the expectation through in order to follow this philosophy of behavior.

I always recommend that at the first sign of trouble, be sure to modify your expectation. In order to hold true to this philosophy, you will have to ensure they complete whatever you say. This is the point of no return. Whatever you say is set in stone, so choose very wisely.

Typically, if I ask them to pick up and I see behaviors beginning, I will modify it to, "Let's each pick up five blocks." Or if they have to do laundry and a behavior begins, modify to, "Why don't you do the wash, and I'll put it in the dryer." By doing this, you are setting up the likelihood of success to be in your favor.

You then say a first/then statement. The "first" is your modified expectation and the "then" is allowing them to escape in the way they are seeking.

For example, "first" pick up five blocks, "then" you can play in the sandbox. Or, "first" load the dishwasher, and "then" you can go back to your game. Compliance is first, and then preference to escape is second. Then, just as with attention-seeking, you are going to wait up to ten minutes (depending on your comfort zone) and continually check in using your same "first/then" phrase.

The ability to escape using inappropriate behavior is quickly learned by children of all ages.

> **Mom:** Can you please put your gym bag in the laundry room?
>
> **Child:** Ugh…why do you make me do everything?
>
> **Mom:** I do not make you do everything. Fine, I'll just do it.

We so often reward disrespect, laziness, and entitlement due to our own convenience. I encourage parents to be careful what you ask them to do. If it's worth asking, it's worth seeing it through.

We then come to behaviors where they are trying to gain something tangible. These types of behaviors are not often long lasting. There are, of course, exceptions to every rule. In my experience, when someone is doing something for attention or an escape, waiting it out and running through the cycles are in your future. With tangible behaviors, they generally peak really quickly, but they also disappear just as quickly.

They will either disappear by providing them the tangible they are seeking (giving them what they want) or we can have a teachable moment. Sure, it may take a tad longer, but the whining, begging, and frequency of tangible-induced behavior will decrease long-term. Stick to your guns and doing it the right way.

To apply our philosophy of behavior to the "tangible" motivator, we would echo:

It is my responsibility to teach them that this tangible seeking behavior no longer gets them this thing. We in essence are teaching them that *things* are a privilege.

By doing this, you are removing the tangible and allowing access only when they are acting appropriately. As far as time limit goes, I'd recommend a minimum of twenty minutes and a maximum of twenty-four hours to remove access to the tangible. Anything shorter than twenty minutes will not require them to feel the cost of their behavior. Anything longer than twenty-four hours will risk losing the understanding or connection between behavior and consequence.

DISCIPLING WITH PURPOSE

By following this discipline guide, the idea is to remove the guesswork, empty threats, negotiations, or frustrated yelling when misbehavior inevitably appears at home or in public. Observe and determine why your child is acting that way, then respond with a consequence that teaches them that misbehavior no longer meets that need. It takes some more brain effort, but goodness, it's a science-backed solution that actually works! The purpose is not to remove personality or self-expression from our kids. Rather, this method is intended to demonstrate the beauty of true love. Love is respectful and honoring to others.

"For the Lord disciplines the one he loves."
Hebrews 12:6

God disciplines us *because* He loves us. His guidelines and boundaries show us that He cares and seeks real time with us not manipulated by ulterior motives like attention-seeking, escaping, or desire for something tangible. When we are disciplining, we should not only be using strategies that work, but doing so because we truly care. If we walk down that road, and discipline out of the care we have for our children, then we will remember the purpose.

Observe and determine why your child

is acting that way, then respond with a

consequence that teaches them that

misbehavior no longer meets that need.

This is as close as we get to a cure to yelling. This is the solution to unrealistic, unhealthy, and illogical consequences thrown out in the heat of the moment. It takes time, patience, and consistency, and our kids are so worth it.

CHAPTER EIGHT

Hard to Find, Lucky to Have

Hard to Find,
Easy to Have.

Every time we braved the outside world, I felt like we came home with something else. My sister and I often joke there's truly nothing more exhausting than having a sick kid. They most certainty do not just sit on the couch and watch a movie like you and I would. I was starting to get into a rhythm though. I learned how to use a ball syringe, which just months prior looked like a completely foreign object to me. I was now moderately informed about which essential oils to use and how to correctly clean and set up the humidifier. I was starting to find a groove to navigate the new world of sick kid. *I'm totally getting this,* I thought.

That was until my sweet six-month-old Zachary got more than just a cold. What started as a cough and sniffles lingered and grew with intensity each day. He had a high fever and wasn't sleeping. After a few more days, he stopped eating completely. Without taking the bottle, we resorted to giving him Pedialyte through a syringe for two days. It wasn't cutting it though, and he became so lethargic we rushed him to the emergency department, where they affirmed he was dehydrated. He lost his voice from crying so much that he just made a whistle noise as the nurses held him down and put in an IV. I was thankful for the intervention, but it absolutely tore my heart out. I found myself in the hallway outside his room desperately trying to hold back my tears.

That same month we went on to have "hand, foot, and mouth" disease, ear infections, bronchitis, an allergic reaction, pink-eye, and we ended it all with the flu. We did this all back to back without a break! You know it's a lot when your pediatrician begins to feel bad for you and asks how you are holding up.

It was a weary blur of a month. The "low fuel" light had gone on days, if not a week ago, yet I still had sick children to care for while being sick myself. Since we were sick, we couldn't be around anyone, which just added to the work load and isolation. I'm a journaler, and some days it's just short ramblings of my life to look back on and remember. During that month, my journal read:

"I am so tired, Lord. I miss interaction, but I really just miss being alone."

It was in that moment I felt the true dichotomy of community in motherhood. The desperate need to surround myself with friends but also the great longing to just rest alone in solitude. God designed us for both. The sheer balance of it all is what can be so tedious and sometimes troublesome. But without it, we lose healthy community.

EXTROVERT HERE!

I would consider myself the extrovert of extroverts. I am naturally recharged by other people. I do not require much time by myself and will often times gravitate towards talking with people over being alone. I can strike up a conversation with pretty much anyone and that excites me. There's even been times in my life that I've neglected solitude and rest for the sake of more community. I just enjoy it that much.

However, there really is something to be said about how becoming mom changes all that. Even I, the extrovert of extroverts, began seeking more and more alone time. I knew I needed to be recharged, but the desire to be all by myself in the quiet sounded like winning the lottery. I cannot express to you how much of a personality shift that was for me. I really started to sympathize and understand my introverted friends! To have a personality that craves solitude in order to be recharged, I couldn't imagine the toll that motherhood must sometimes play. Motherhood does not come with much built-in time away, and not knowing if or when that alone time will come can be a real difficult thing.

Even if our personalities stayed the same after kids, our needs might have shifted—whether we like it or not. What I mean by that is moms need friends. Everyone needs community, but we're going to get more specific with it. Whether you prefer your own space, prefer the shared space of company, or just take what you can get—moms need a village of help. Like taking a Sabbath, friendship is not an "if I have time" luxury, nor should it be something we put off until we feel like we meet the mom standards we imposed on ourselves. Like food, water, and sleep, we are required to incorporate companionship into our balance.

As our Mom Mode clicks on and the everyday feels harder, we probably need community the most, yet that can be when we're most inclined to recline on the couch and eat the feelings instead. I know I felt this way. How does it work to have adult friends in life after kids, though? The recliner has no schedule, no agenda, and I think it's safe to say I win the beauty contest, so I don't feel very insecure around it.

BE A FRIEND

The Bible tells us that we need other people. One of my favorite illustrations of needing others comes from when Paul talks about the parts of the body.

> *"For the body does not consist of one member but of many. If the foot should say, 'Because I am not a hand, I do not belong to the body,' that would not make it any less a part of the body. And if the ear should say, 'Because I am not an eye, I do not belong to the body,' that would not make it any less a part of the body. If the whole body were an eye, where would be the sense of hearing? If the whole body were an ear, where would be the sense of smell? But as it is, God arranged the members in the body, each one of them, as he chose. If all were a single member, where would the body be? As it is, there are many parts, yet one body."*
> 1 Corinthians 12:14-20

When we avoid community for the sake of excessive solitude, we are forfeiting our full value. We are not living our full potential to be everything God made us to be. The body works because it's operating together. Every part giving. Every part benefiting. We are made complete when we are living this giving-and-benefiting ebb and flow together. When we share both the highs and lows of our days. When we ask for advice and also provide input for others. When we laugh and have fun, but also when we come together to sob, punch pillows, or stare at the wall. Living life together allows us to operate within God's design. Relying on one another's gift and also contributing. Both benefiting and sacrificing for friendship.

There was a study that was conducted by the University of Tennessee that really stood out to me, though. This study included 1,082 mother-and-child pairs. What they found

When we avoid community for the sake of excessive solitude, we are forfeiting our full value. We are not living our full potential to be everything God made us to be.

was that mothers who had wide social circles had children that were positively affected.[17] The social mama's children had better cognitive development. The opportunities they saw as "just another play date" actually exposed their child to new experiences and interactions they otherwise wouldn't have. These experiences would go on to have a positive effect on their growing brains. How amazing is that?

Getting together with friends is not only beneficial for you; it's for your children too. They get to see how other people live, play, and speak. They are exposed to different values and lifestyles. Goodness, it's just as beneficial for us to see too. We can learn right alongside our children that people are different than us, and that another world exists outside ours. People have different rules, expectations, and interests. We can value and learn from this diversity and outside perspective.

WHAT'S HOLDING US BACK

Being a friend requires great vulnerability. This comes easier for some than others. Some of you need to place a great amount of effort and intentionality to be open and vulnerable with others. This means that for you to share what is actually going on in life—things that you are struggling with and ask for advice—is something that makes you uncomfortable. As long as you make an effort to be open and to continue even if one time doesn't feel or go perfect, there is nothing wrong with it not coming naturally. That's just your personality. The reason I encourage you to really keep at it is to avoid giving up on sharing. What this results in is having just one friend that you confide everything in. As a result, you demand everything from this one person.

Whether you see it or not, having limited friendships puts strain on that relationship. There is a natural dependency and burden that can easily begin to form if you are not careful.

You begin to expect them to have the answers to all of your questions *since they are your only friend.*

You begin to expect them to always show up for you *since they are your only friend.*

You begin to expect too much from them *since they are your only friend.*

We were not intended to just have one or two friends, but sadly research also supports that this is often times the case for moms. We struggle making and keeping friends. The data is very clear on this. If you only have a one or two friends, you are actually in the majority. Friendships as an adult are difficult no matter what way you slice it. It's not as easy or convenient as it once was.

Another major obstacle to our lack of friendship circles is simply lack of time. We are either a working mom, and time is non-existent as long as our kids are existent. Maybe you are homeschooling, so all your time is poured into finding a way to balance housework, schoolwork, and motherhood. It's difficult to maintain a relationship with someone that you are not talking to frequently.

I can confirm time and schedules are overwhelming when trying to make and keep friends, and none of the solutions are cure-all medicines. But don't give up yet.

EXPECTATIONS CHANGE, FRIENDS DON'T

Community starts with changing our expectations. The way friendship looks will change. However, just because the appearance of friendships change does not mean that we have to give it up altogether.

The importance is not so much with the *frequency* of visiting necessarily, but more the *intentionality* of setting aside some time. Prior to becoming a mom, you probably got together and physically saw your friends more often. How often and consistently you visit with friends likely changed when you welcomed kids into the world. Truthfully, I do not have as many friends since being a mom, but my true friendships have improved since motherhood. They are the ones who I allow to see me when I haven't showered in four days and when my house is a mess. They are the ones who I've shared my darkest fears with. They are ultimately the ones who I know really care about me. I know this because even though we are not able to get together often, we both put forth a lot of effort to keep the relationship going.

If your life looks like that exhausting month of sickness in my house, it makes a lot of sense that your first thought is the couch or bed. You yearn for solitude, but deep down, you know you should pick up the phone. Time alone too often will not meet the need of comfort and female companionship in your heart. I think if we are honest with ourselves, we will be able to tell when it's time.

The rules seem to shift a bit when it comes to making friends as an adult. When we were younger, friends were an obvious necessity. If we didn't have friends, we felt as if we couldn't survive! As an adult, we don't mind quiet Saturday nights so much.

The importance is not so much with the frequency
of visiting necessarily, but more the intentionality of
setting aside some time.

We convince ourselves it's not as much of a need, when really it may be a need more than ever.

When the "making friends" part feels like the most confusing step, try attending and greeting people at a church, a Moms of Preschoolers (MOPS) group, or try a Bible study. Or you can sign up for a class at the park district, take on a group hobby, join a gym, or head to the playground and boldly introduce yourself to other moms! In my experience, if you head anywhere that kids are welcome, you'll find people just like you—in this strollers and backpacks stage of life—also ready and willing to make a friend.

MAKE A FRIEND, BE A FRIEND

When you begin to break free from your comfort zone and focus on friendship, I'd challenge you to ensure that you are meeting people who are of varying ages, personalities, backgrounds, interests, and associations to avoid a friendship bubble. The byproduct of friendship is unity, not uniformity. It's human nature to gravitate toward similarity and reject those that look, act, and think differently than you. I believe we do this partially because diversity takes more effort. I can guarantee diversity in friendship is completely worth it though.

The toxic perversion of friendship diversity tends to prevent, moms, are cliques. A clique is a group of "friends" who are exclusive to one another and hence not welcoming and warm. Sometimes they're not even welcoming and warm to each other! They checked their "number of friends I need" box and they are not interested in adding anybody else. Either that, or they are interested in including you only if you look and act like them. The "you can join our club as long as you follow our set of unspoken rules" mentality is not really a friendship.

Sometimes our friend circles morph to be cliques. It happens so slowly that we don't see the transformation. We don't want to believe it happens either. That's a high school thing! Like I said, though, it's natural for us to surround ourselves with people who look and think like us. It's just easier. So even if we are not intentionally creating or enabling a clique, it happens more often than we want to believe. Friendships with people who are different than us challenge us and help us grow. Friendships with people who are just like us help us stay right where we are.

DIFFERENT POSTURES OF FRIENDSHIP

There are five different types of friends I'd like to suggest you connect with on this new friendship adventure I'm sending you on.

The first type of friend I'd like for you to meet is what we'll refer to as the *Everyday Mama*. This is the mom friend you to see most often and are doing your day-to-day life with. She is often in the same season of life as you, and she has similar values and interests. She most likely has children the same age as yours, and you are able to get together to do many activities. You talk to her frequently. You connect on a peer level. You are both giving and receiving in this relationship. You do not view one as being higher—you're both in the trenches!

This is a back-and-forth relationship. This person is someone who gives you true fellowship. You feel most comfortable around them. You can count on them to tell you how it is. You trust their guidance and know they will always encourage you to be your best.

Having an everyday mom friend is light and sweet to the soul. It brings a level of companionship that is fulfilling and restful. Having a person you can text a funny kid quote to (or the picture of your embarrassing mom fail) is having the security and assurance that someone cares and knows what's going on in your house these days. Someone that is not your family or husband. Someone who relates to you on a motherhood level. This type of person is one that we most often picture when we think of community. They make life more interesting and motherhood less lonely.

Next, I'd like for you to meet the *Mentor Mama*. This is a person you may have had a friendship with prior, yet you look up to her in a particular area of her expertise. She may be gifted in the area of cooking, breastfeeding, or working out—and you go to her for help. This person could also be someone who you had no previous relationship with. You sought her out initially because of her expertise. In either case, this is a person who is a friend now. They are not a professional that you hire and chat with on the weekend. This is a friendship; however, you receive more than you give.

Not all relationships will be an equal give-and-take like the *Everyday Mama* friendship, and that is completely okay. This friendship is one that focuses more on what the other woman is gifted in and is willing to give. Chances are others have recognized her gift in this area and she's playing the *Mentor Mama* friendship in others' lives as well. You are going to her for direction, support, accountability, and guidance on a particular topic.

Sometimes this friend is older. Sometimes her children are already grown, and you are seeking the wisdom of motherhood from someone who has already been there and reached the finish line in some ways. Scripture tells us this model of asking an older woman who has been there for advice is a helpful thing (Titus 2:4). Sometimes this friend is a peer, not a mom, and they are just really gifted in a particular topic.

When Zachary was really sick and he stopped eating, I was at an absolute loss. I didn't have the slightest clue how to respond. As always, I took out my phone and desperately tried searching for answers. I thankfully had an awakening in the middle of it all.

Why am I asking Google rather than a trusted friend?

I paused, thought of a friend who was in the medical field, and gave them a call. Wouldn't you know, they were pleased to be able to walk me through my next steps. I've found people are more than willing to help as long as they are clear that is what you are after. I'd encourage you to be as clear as possible. Use statements such as "Hey, I'd love to learn from you. Can I talk to you sometimes about _____?"

You can also be the *Mentor Mama* for another person, but that will only be possible after you befriend the *Younger Mama*. In this friendship you are giving more than you are getting. This is, once again, not a give-and-take relationship. You are stepping into the role of guiding, directing, helping, and assisting another along. Maybe it is guidance on how to do something, or maybe it's life advice in general. Either way, when this friend needs help, you lead them.

In my experience, sometimes I'll come across someone who just pricks my heart. They generally have a piece of my story within theirs, and initiates a strong bond. For me, whenever I hear someone is encountering adoption struggles, I'm all in to help. That's where my passion is. I remember being the *only one* in my circle of friends experiencing adoption, and while they were sympathetic, they didn't relate when my psych report wasn't accepted for my Dossier, or when I had another post-report due. Rightfully so— they never lived that story. When I see someone who is on that path, I always offer to help. Even if it's just a listening ear, I know I have something to offer them.

You too are gifted and passionate in an area. I know there is some because that makes your heart ache as well. Maybe you had a premature child or spent time in the NICU. Maybe you struggled with health concerns while caring for young children. Maybe you know how to lose that extra baby weight and regain your strength. You have something you can offer someone else. When you step into a friendship with the goal to help, you walk away blessed and filled. You are assured that God had a plan for your gifts and story, and you see the potential of their ending as well.

Lastly, we all need a friend who is *Not A Mama*. Yep, you heard me correctly. Someone who is not waste-deep in Cheerios. If they don't have kids, they meet the criteria. You may think this is an odd request, but hear me out. Sometimes when we live in our Mommy world, we get some serious tunnel vision. All you see is kids and mamas. That's a pretty limited perspective! You don't see the outside world where people are living very different lives. They are not cleaning up food that was rubbed in the carpet. They are not chasing a half-naked child around. You laugh, but I promise you there is a huge chunk of women out there not living your reality.

Find a friend who doesn't get it. As lovely as being a mom is, these friends remind us who we are outside of our kids. They appreciate who we are as women, as professionals, as believers, as creatives, and anything else we sometimes feel or don't realize gets buried under "Mama."

I have a good friend who is not a mother. She loves to hear my stories. She buys my kids birthday and Christmas presents. She comes over and braves my sticky floor often. Yet, she does not relate. Let me tell you, though. She is one of my closest and dearest friends. She keeps me grounded. *Not a Mama* friends do not take away from our motherhood. They actually enhance it. Mine allows me to understand my purpose even more clearly. That is a person that will challenge you and encourage you in ways that will catch you by surprise.

TRUE REFRESHMENT

There is a newer trend in recent years where a future dad and future mom take one "last hurrah" of a trip before their baby comes and changes their lives. It's called a baby-moon, and I think it's a cute concept. We struggled with infertility for ten years, so we had plenty of time to go on vacation.

We do look back today though and just laugh at the amount of freedom we once had. Every year, we would go on a vacation for our anniversary. We were "double income, no kids" (DINKS) and living life to the fullest. What did we need a vacation from? Not really sure now that I look back on it. As I write this, one of those vacations actually sounds quite nice.

One of my favorite vacations we took was a cruise to the Caribbean. It was beautiful. We would port in a new country each day, where we could enjoy the beautiful beaches, then at night, we'd catch a live band.

One particular day, we ported in the Bahamas. We packed our bags with sunscreen, extra clothes, and all the things we thought we'd need that day. The beach was breath-taking. The water was crystal blue. There was hardly anyone on the sand. It was blazing hot—exactly the way we love it! Everything was perfect until we started sweating and getting dehydrated. We didn't pack any water. We just assumed there would be a place to purchase some.

We walked tiki hut to tiki hut on the beach, but everyone said they only had alcohol. Nobody had water! Here we were, on one of the most beautiful beaches in the world, having access to unlimited extras and delicacies, completely parched. We didn't have the basic necessity of water, which made all the extras unenjoyable. It didn't matter how beautiful the place was or how extravagant the day could have been; we just remember having sand-paper mouths and craving something so simple. Something we could have gotten out of our sink if we were back home.

Are you ready for another Proverb?

"A sweet friendship refreshes the soul."
Proverbs 27:9 msg

Just as we craved the water to refresh us on that hot day, our soul craves community and nothing else can imitate it. You can have the hubby, the kids, the house, the car, the vacations, and that cute little puppy that make your family seem complete, but without fellowship, your faith and mental health will suffer. It doesn't matter if you have everything else going for you. If you have nobody to share it with, you will be like our beach day.

To the mamas reading this with that cotton-mouth thirst and seemingly nowhere to find water, I see you. You're thirsty for friends and can't seem to figure it out. I'm so sorry if you feel alone right now. Keep your head up.

I'd encourage you to pivot perspectives. Instead of seeing yourself as the person without any water among so many tiki huts, be the resource of water for someone else. Pray for God to reveal others around you who need the gifts you have, and for wisdom as you meet and connect with them. It will most likely be uncomfortable to take the leap into the adult-friend pool, as the water there is chopping and uninviting at times. I promise you it's worth the plunge. There are a lot of great people in the world that will make life and motherhood a lot more fun. Allow yourself the temporary discomfort to find people who refresh your soul.

CHAPTER NINE

Mom Mode

Sometimes I wonder if animals in the wild ever struggle with burnout. Do they get headaches? Feel tired? The requirement of food, water, and safety demand they remain on their feet, resting in much different patterns than we do. Humans are really the only creatures I can think of that experience burnout, which can be the result of overexertion, over-commitment, a string of unfortunate events, an unhealthy work environment, and any number of other factors.

As mothers, burnout is often triggered by the nonstop demands of our energetic younglings. Our brains lose power among the shrill and needless crying; many half-drank cups of milk; trails of toys; pieces of puzzles you know you'll be looking for in a few days; hours of loading, chauffeuring, and unloading complicated car seats; meal planning and grocery shopping within budgets; laundry; enforcement of screen time rules; unhealthy snack patrol; and managing the balance of entertaining them and letting them whine when each has different wants and attention spans. These little chores are not hard on their own, nor were they unexpected, but without a break in between or reasonable expectations for what a day is supposed to be used for, they initiate the Mom Mode in the brain. A dense fog of exhaustion, dissociation, and physical weariness often accompanied with an attitude that if we just get all our things done, it'll go away.

AS COMMON AS A COLD

At some point, people accepted it's more or less just a way of life. Moms will be overwhelmed. Sometimes we laugh about it, or at other times complain. What happens though is that we don't actually sit down and discuss with other moms what to do with this debilitating mental state and the long "to-do list" we create to remedy it.

Maybe we think it's because we are the only one that doesn't have everything together.

> *If I were more efficient, I wouldn't be stuck thinking about all the things I still need to accomplish before I go to bed tonight.*

Maybe we don't want to bother others with our problems.

> *I'd open up and share I'm struggling but they wouldn't understand. They clearly have everything all together.*

Perhaps you are just so consumed by your list that you don't even have time to think about what to do with it long-term. Goodness, you are trying to just make it to lunchtime.

If we don't make time for a real solution, Mom Mode leads to a place of almost idolatry—not because you want to worship chores but because the to-dos end up coming before everything else, robbing you of your original and pure intent to serve and meet the physical needs surrounding your children and household.

Mom Mode occurs when the chatter in your mind becomes so clouded and muddy that you begin to easily drift towards self-sufficiency. This may be because you do everything yourself—it's easier than to explain what needs to be done or ask for help. Or maybe you begin skipping important communication that needs to take place because you forget who you told what to when.

Our shoulders are much too delicate for all the weight we try to carry. We cannot do everything every day for everyone, but sometimes we still try our gosh-darn hardest. When our kids, our neighbors, our friends, our schools, our family, or our church ask us for time or resources, we choose "yes" because a "no" might invite a "why not?" And answering that means admitting we are not Wonder Woman and that we may actually be crumbling.

I know I've been guilty of setting my mom standards sky-high, only to be left feeling like I've been hit by a truck. It's not like this is a one-time occurrence either. Whenever I'm able to magically meet the end of my list and keep up with it for a while, I figure the Mom Mode I fought for four days was just a rough patch. No big deal. I got through it and now I'm good. But when we experience Mom Mode, it should act as a warning

Mom Mode occurs when the chatter in your mind becomes so clouded and muddy that you begin to easily drift towards self-sufficiency.

signal. That's a warning to pay attention. We're setting expectations for our brains and bodies that we will not be able to sustainably meet.

WHAT WE RISK

When Mom Mode is activated, we lose sight of the people we are serving, and we begin to just see tasks. The process to complete the task doesn't matter, and the focus becomes on the completion itself. The physical need demanding our attention must be completed at all costs. This can be anything from dishes, carpooling, homework, or grocery shopping. The signs are feelings of being rushed, impatient, and insensitive. We begin to find more value in completion than of character. Those beautiful check marks beside the day's tasks become our idol.

The more we praise the check marks, though, the more we will see the damage. By choosing completion over character, we reproduce what we've become. Our children's character will also become compromised as they see tasks over the beauty of being in the moment, experiencing joy, and living out of a place of contentment. Even before that happens, the constant rush to get everything done might create anxiety and guilt within our kids as they perceive their needs as inconveniences or associate them with a dip in our mood. Human nature pulls us into extremes which is why a fundamental truth of healthy living—mentally, spiritually, physically, emotionally, nutritionally, financially, etc.—is *everything in moderation.* We represent this for our kids, so while creating lists and teaching them to help with chores is a valuable part of instilling responsibility, so is exemplifying flexibility, respect for ourselves and each other, and fun!

Sometimes deeper issues drive Mom Mode than simply burnout.

Identity is certainly a possible reason why mothers lose their alertness and shift into task mode. I know just this week alone I was stuck in the gear of Mom Mode. I justified why I was so busy, naming what must be done and how I'm the only one who can do it! What really happened, though, was I took on way too much because I don't always trust that being "Mom" is enough, and I want to do more and more to prove my worth.

In other circumstances, I'm guilty of people-pleasing. Am I a victim of this mental state because I really had to do it all or because I said yes to win someone's approval? To avoid feeling guilty for letting them down? We want to be wanted and needed, and we don't want that to go away. Of course we're going to say yes! The risk of someone not asking us for help another time is too scary.

One other reason I want to mention—motherhood comes with little appreciation at times. It's mundane. Sometimes being a mom can become a *Groundhog's Day* situation, every day the same! That is when we begin to look for the next best thing. When we do the *extras,* we experience newness. We feel uplifted. Volunteering at the church vacation Bible school is at least something different. We are not complete, happy, financially secure, or fulfilled without *that* thing. But we end up sacrificing our happiness in the pursuit of happiness!

Moms who don't put down their to-do lists, let their brains rest, and spend undistracted time with their kids can fall into an even more dangerous coping mechanism than housework and kid duties. When the check marks no longer validate or soothe the perpetual haze of burnout, we turn to our own emotions to call the shots. Our rest-deprived emotions will take the lead in determining what will make us feel better, and it's usually at the expense of others' feelings. Our emotion grows larger and larger, while the needs of our children, our spouse, or our household become smaller.

HOW ABOUT AN EXAMPLE?

Imagine a cute, active, third-grade boy who hadn't completed his book report due tomorrow. A tale as old as time…

This frustrated Mom. Dad communicated with Mom and Son that morning that he will help Son with the procrastinated homework. However, Dad doesn't get home until five, and when Son gets home at three, Mom sees Son playing and grows more frustrated. Because Mom is struggling with a "Mom Mode" mentality, her emotions promise her:

"Once the book report is done, you will stop being so frustrated with your son."

She does not like this ugly emotion she feels toward her child, and she wants to get rid of it. On a normal day, a book report would not be so stressful. This was a teaching moment, not a call for severe discipline.

Mom planned to use the task (the book report) to stop feeling the ugly emotion (frustration and anger). She believed once the book report was finished, the tension with her son about procrastinating on the deadline, as well as playing outside while he waited for Dad, will magically disappear. Once her son sat and completed the book report, the anger would surely go away.

When Dad and Son work on the book report all night and Mom did other chores that Dad and Son typically helped with, she felt a little less frustrated about the book report.

Mom tried to make these feelings in herself go away by putting pressure on the task to resolve them. However, even though her son completed the book report and had a meaningful talk about homework with Dad, Mom's emotions will not have been processed in a healthy and self-reflective manner. When frustration comes back, the emotion will once again place pressure on a task to alleviate it.

MOMS, NOT MARTYRS

We might meet our physical needs and our family's while in Mom Mode, but in a hostile, rushed, or annoyed manner about the tasks brought our way. The struggle to let go of control and hold on to relationships is hard in Mom Mode. We do not have the capacity or energy needed to focus on what God tells us to be true. Thus, we become internally focused on "fixing" our emotional distress, and we turn our focus on ourselves.

One of the easiest ways to prevent and alleviate Mom Mode is giving yourself permission to say "no" more and "yes" less. The answer isn't shocking. It's obvious and really quite simple. But that doesn't make it easy, particularly in the moment.

Knowing when we should say "yes" and when we should say "no" is a matter of discernment. There are no hard-and-fast rules I can share with you on this one. What might exhaust me more might not be the same for you, and therefore what we decline and accept depends.

What is universal, and something that all moms can work towards unanimously is balance. Again, everything in moderation, mamas. Mental and emotional steadiness. It's the internal state of being able to cope with the expectations before you.

> *A false balance is an abomination to the Lord,*
> *but a just weight is his delight.*
> **Proverbs 11:1**

It's God's delight that you have balance because He knows that you will have delight when you find balance.

Imagine you were taking a tour of the Grand Canyon, but you were riding a donkey on one of those skinny trails. When you arrived at the bottom, someone asked you about the bubbling creek you passed. Would you be able to describe it? My guess is no. You probably didn't see anything but the skinny path. Your focus was on keeping your balance so you wouldn't fall (or cause the donkey to fall). Now, if you were to tour the Grand Canyon and walked down with ease, you probably would have not only taken in the beautiful sights of the creek and landscape, but the setting sun and rock formations as well. You could see the beauty around you and enjoy the moment because you had the clarity to focus.

Our brain is only able to see beauty when it feels safe enough.

FILTERING THE NOISE

In the 1950s, Donald Broadbent argued that our minds have a "filter." He agreed that our mind processes many thoughts at once, but that we truly could only *focus* on one thought at a time. He coined the term the "cocktail party effect" to represent the concept.[18] The example that Broadbent used to describe the theory was how we can focus on one conversation in the midst of a loud, chaotic cocktail party. We can hear the music, see the dancers, eavesdrop on the conversation next to us—those are all things we are processing. However, when engaging with others, we can only have one conversation at a time. We must choose what we focus on in the midst of the chaotic party. We take in the whole party, but we are focused on just one thing.

If you are experiencing a life that is too full, too packed, and off-balance, you will be taking in the surroundings but unable to retain it or enjoy the moment. You will be taking your focus off the things that truly matter, instead honing in on the thought that has held your beautiful brain captive in Mom Mode.

God recognizes there are needs that require our attention. That is why he talks about a *"just weight."* He knows there will be weight to hold. The problem isn't the tasks, nor is the solution to say "no" to *every* responsibility outside the scope of motherhood. The goal here is to ensure we can balance the load that is on our plate. Just because we are doing it all doesn't mean we do it well or sustainably. Just because we are "checking all the boxes" doesn't mean we are really eliminating any boxes, nor are we necessarily improving our mental and emotional stability.

Some examples of being off-balance could be dedicating too much time to volunteering at the school which leads us to not be available to cook or even eat dinner together anymore. We've overcommitted ourselves to church so that we are now unable to help

Just because we are "checking all the boxes" doesn't mean we are really eliminating any boxes, nor are we necessarily improving our mental and emotional stability.

with homework. We are rushing through bath time and end up screaming at the kids, but it's only because we were answering e-mails that probably should have waited for tomorrow morning.

Volunteering, serving, and working are all good things. But we cannot be everything for everyone all the time. Our mom role is a large one. It's a validated hard gig.

If you find yourself always living off-balance, always feeling limited by time and frequently experiencing Mom Mode, I'd first ask if this is a choice or a necessity? Is this something that you need to do, something you'd like to do, or something others tell you that you should do? It's really easy to justify why you *need* to do something. I think you'd be surprised, when you really sit down and try to explain what is grabbing for your time, how much of it is an obligation we've placed on ourselves rather than a need.

We all come with different expectations and requirements. Mom Mode is not a good forever plan for life, and that's why the continuous art of balance is worthy of our attention. There are seasons when we must do things. If you find this lasts longer than expected, or has no clear end in sight, I'd encourage you to reach out to someone. Find a pastor, friend, or counselor who can help you navigate your schedule and needs. You should not have to live in a constant state of instability. Absolutely, there will be busy seasons where Mom Mode makes an appearance. Let's just recognize it and put guard-rails up to ensure its short-term and not forever.

ALL THE THINGS

We *all* have brains that flick the switch to Mom Mode. We all drift towards this state of mind. Sometimes the circumstances are out of our control. Other times, I worry it's more self-inflicted. We take on too much because it's what we know how to do. It's not an abundant way to live, but it's comfortable, so we choose to stay for a while. Even when we have opportunities to get help, weeks with little on our plates, or ample grace to say "no" to commitments, we invite the overwhelm anyway.

The psychologist Robert Zajonc discovered and dug into this concept of preferring what is familiar.[19] Zajonc engaged in studies demonstrating a strong correlation that people chose preference to things that were familiar to them. They might not have truly preferred the object, but simply because they saw it once or twice prior, they chose that as their favorite.

We do not enjoy being in a state of chaos. When we have overcommitted ourselves (for whatever reason), we are left frustrated and maybe even telling ourselves we are not going to do this to ourselves ever again. We convince ourselves to *take it easy* next week or even back out of a commitment to lessen our load. The next day though, once the dust has settled, we can be off piling things back on to our schedule.

We drift towards what we've always done, because newness is hard. Change is difficult. People are hard-wired to lean toward familiarity. Sometimes we grow so accustomed to being busy that we no longer take notice or remember that's not a healthy homeostasis. Being energized and available makes us uncomfortable! What do we do?!

There is a commercial that really cracks me up. I don't even remember what they are advertising, but there is a lady sitting on a couch. This dingy, nasty-looking couch is covered with dog hair. You obviously can't smell what she smells through the television, but the visceral image emits a stench anyway. The owner of the couch, the lady sitting on it, doesn't seem to mind though. She has become "nose-blind." She doesn't even realize the couch stinks because after so long around the smell, and slowly sitting longer and longer on the couch, it becomes normal.

The "stinky couch" in our world is the mindset of constantly working and moving. I'm sure we can remember that first experience or two at college, at a job, or trying to pay bills where we realized being an adult is not fun! Growing up is exhausting, and everyone else just nods and says, "Get used to it." First it was one tough day, then week, until every day was easier if we just looked at the day like a list.

We operate from an unstable, unfocused, and unproductive mindset for so long that we don't even take notice anymore. We accept it as "something that comes with the job," laugh about it with other mom friends, or brush it off completely so much that we justify its effects.

HOW AM I DOING, REALLY?

I've started doing a morning check in. There is no magic formula within the questions that I use, so feel free to develop and amend the ones that I propose. The purpose of the check-in is just staying in touch with reality and in touch with what "mode" I'm in.

Inevitably, the day will bring many things that require your attention. What I find, however, is that if we carry something unstable from the day prior into the beginning of a new day, we will never be able to keep up. We need to do business with whatever is causing our emotional and mental unrest before more is added on.

The questions that I ask myself are reflective.

First, is there anything on my mind that I need to address? If there is something bothering you, come up with a plan on when you will think more on it or contact the person. If you just continually carry that around with you, I guarantee you'll experience Mom Mode. You will be leaving a box in your mind open indefinitely, and your brain doesn't like open boxes.

Follow that up with some other questions, like what do I have to give to God this morning? I come back to this verse time and time again:

> *"Cast all your anxieties on him, because he cares for you."*
> 1 PETER 5:7

God cares so much for us and knows that we will live emotionally unbalanced lives if we carry our "open-boxed" items around with us all day long. I mean, He designed our brains. He knows that's not how they were built to operate. We need to unload and dump the excess worries we have on Him. The text says He commands us to do this because He cares for us so much. Each day is a gift from Him, and the worries from previous days spoil the gift before we can even unwrap it. So, say a prayer each morning. Write it in a journal. Do whatever you have to do in order to get it out.

God wants you to put it on Him. He wants you to leave it for Him to work through. I'd encourage you to end with asking yourself this third question:

What do I need to do to complete the tasks ahead of me today with joy?

Do you need to make a deal with yourself? It's totally acceptable to treat yourself to Starbucks—I'm just saying…

Those are built-in reinforcers that motivate us to do the hard work. That's okay. Rewards do not have to be reserved for our children alone.

That time of morning reflection has been a game changer for me. They may sound like three simple questions, and they are, but it leads to a mind of clarity. It allows me to continue my day in control of my mind rather than overtaken by Mom Mode.

You too can have clarity. You can break free from the thoughts that hold your mind captive and rob you of your motherhood joy. Addressing the fog and taking your mind back is worth the effort, and you will find freedom in all the beautiful moments you'll start noticing.

CHAPTER TEN

Anxious Mamas

Anxious Minds

woke up one the morning and I couldn't open my hands. I didn't even know this was possible, but I slept all night clenching my fists. Trying to start the day, I was speechless with pain. I felt like I was a hundred years old and just slammed my hands in a car door fifty times.

Let me back up.

The day before was really stressful. We were getting ready to go on a family vacation. While this was supposed to be fun, travel prep is a lot more complicated with young kids. It takes effort to have fun in the chaos. This particular vacation, we were flying. We had car seats, luggage, and a stroller. I'm big enough to admit we were the people you do *not* want to be behind.

The real kicker for me was that I do not like to fly. My nerves were already on overdrive. Drake required a breathing treatment before getting into the air. Then, right before we boarded, my sister called to say her dog had been poisoned. This added to my stress, fueling my anxious feelings on the plane. I was concerned for my sister, I felt guilty I wasn't there for her, and I was distracted and absent-minded writing potential endings to the scenario when I should have been focused on the hectic travel plans. We arrived safely, but it wasn't the start of the "fun" vacation I went in expecting.

By the time we actually made it to our hotel safely (praise God), I was spent. We gave my son a final treatment, I checked in on my sister, and we all fell asleep. I was emotionally and physically exhausted. Hence, I must have slept all night long clenching my fists, my body inhaling all the worry and fear without any means to exhale.

It wasn't as obvious to me then, but I struggle with feelings of anxiety. I hate that I do,

I try with all my might to just *not feel this way* anymore. It wasn't until I began digging through the literature on anxiety from a professional standpoint that I realized my own personal wrestling match with it. I must say, with some interventions, I have found some relief—and I thankfully haven't fallen asleep clenching my hands in a while. Allow me to share.

DEFINING THE UNDEFINABLE

Anxiety means something different to different people. Clinically, it's a condition. Socially, it's a spectrum of emotion. To those who struggle with it, it's a nightmare. It is both something everyone feels occasionally and something others experience chronically.

In some ways, psychologists and those who have experienced it still can't say we really know what it is.

You may be *Mom A*, who says, "I have anxiety." You have a diagnosed anxiety disorder, and/or are taking anti-anxiety medication, and/or are currently (or have in the past) received therapeutic intervention for your anxiety. I in no way want to minimize the fact that there is a physiological component that drives anxiety. Based on our experienced, learned behavior, and genetic makeup, some of you may be predisposition to thinking and acting out of an abundance of anxiety despite the hard work you've put in to cope otherwise. I see you, and I want you to know that you are not broken, and there is hope for your anxiety to improve.

You may be *Mom B*, who says, "I think I have anxiety." This is the mom who does things that she doesn't want to do, or she doesn't do things that she wants to do out of anxious feelings. You do not have a diagnosed disorder, but there is a battleground in your mind and a war in your emotions.

Maybe you are *Mom C*, who says, "I don't have anxiety." I have spoken to women before who join me in my virtual office and share that they always identified as a person who didn't struggle with anxiety until they became a mom. There is just something about the responsibility of raising another little human that brings out fear and anxious feelings. Maybe you want to become *Mom C* again and ditch your new anxiety struggle. The hope is that you can say this isn't a war you battle regularly.

For the purpose and strategies we'll discuss today, we are going to define anxiety as believing and meditating on half-truths, which cause us an emotional dysregulation, ultimately leading to a physical response, which will lead us to act differently.

Okay, I know that's complex. That is the thing about anxiety though: it's not easy to

Anxiety means something different to different people. Clinically, it's a condition. Socially, it's a spectrum of emotion. To those who struggle with it, it's a nightmare.

explain or define. We'll break this down together, but I want you to know that this is for the average mom who is struggling with anxiety. If you need additional support—more than this chapter provides—I would encourage you to reach out to a professional when you are finished reading to chat further.

Our anxious thoughts and feelings affect us in different ways and to different degrees, but one thing that Moms A, B, and C all have in common is the power to make improvements. We can lessen our symptoms. We can identify unhealthy thinking patterns. We can make changes to the way we respond. We may not all have the power to get rid of our anxiety, but we can dedicate ourselves to improvement.

ANXIETY IS MYSTERIOUS

Anxiety has a lot of power, and can rightfully be described as a villainous mastermind. It takes you captive before you see where it came from. That is why many report feelings of anxiety but cannot begin to identify the root cause.

I like to ask clients or groups this question: "What is the root of anxiety?"

I'll even make this a multiple-choice test and provide them some options.

"Is anxiety rooted in the mind, emotions, actions, or our biology?"

The answer, moms, is your *mind*. Anxiety absolutely will go on to affect every one of the options (emotions, actions, and our body). That is what makes that test so difficult. Anxiety affects all four areas of our lives, but it will originate within our thoughts. Anxiety is a battleground of the mind.[20]

After pulling back the curtain on anxiety's methods, it's clearer how it works. It begins with a thought that I like to define as a "half-truth." This is something that has a seed of truth, but that we take out of context.

After your thoughts are affected, it will then affect your emotions and your body. You will begin to feel worried, frustrated, and panicked. When your thought connects with your emotion, it will cause a physiological reaction. You will be sending a message to your body that you need to respond. Your body might become impaired as your heart beats faster, you breathe shallower and quickly, and/or sweat on your palms.

The last area affected is your actions. If you choose to give in to anxiety, then it also affects what you do. It's there that anxiety really has taken you captive. Anxiety (which began with a half-truth) has now taken over your mind, emotions, body, and actions. It now has you acting out its plans.

Let me share with you a silly personal example so that we can walk through the method of anxiety. I really dislike (okay, maybe hate) driving over bridges. For me, it begins with the half-truth that the bridge could fall. It's a half-truth because have bridges fallen in the past? Yes, they have. Will the bridge fall that I'm on though? Probably not. What I've done is taken something that has a seed of truth and made it a much more likely possibility in my brain. I engaged in a half-truth, which originated in my mind. This half-truth then caused an emotional response of fear. When my thought and emotions (I'm terrified!) come together, it signals my body to respond. Cue my heart pounding and my breathing becoming labored. Lastly, my actions will ultimately follow. My son could be in the backseat trying to tell me something, but I am not listening. I am avoiding conversation because I am acting on my half-truth, which is anxiety's ploy.

ANXIETY IS BROAD

The half-truths that we believe, mediate on, and ponder vary vastly from mom to mom. What one mother struggles to recognize as not really something to be concerned with, another can easily let go, and it's typically based on what factors we tend to fixate upon. Cognitive Behavior Therapy, which is a form of psychological treatment for anxiety and depression, labels these factors "thinking traps." These are traps that get us to believe half-truths.

In addition to *Catastrophizing* (focusing on the worst-case scenario) like my bridge example, there's a one called *All-or-Nothing*. This thinking trap says "it must be perfect or it's not worth doing at all."

At its root, this is a mom who struggles with perfectionism. We all desire to have the Pinterest-worthy birthday parties, house, and wardrobe, but for this mom, it's not a desire as much as a need. If you are this mom, you may suffer from fatigue trying to keep up with the unrealistic expectations that you've placed on yourself. They could be heard saying things such as:

"They can't come here because my house isn't clean."

"I don't fit in the dress I wanted to wear, so I'm not going to go."

"No, we can't take a picture, I didn't do my makeup today."

When something doesn't go as planned, someone stuck in an All-or-Nothing think-ing trap has the temptation to pull out completely. They would rather have no part of it than show their flaws. They may "have it all together" on the outside, but I can guess that behind the perfection is a mom who is deeply crippled with anxiety.

I know it can be difficult as you feel you cannot function in the unknown. You put on "perfect" because the idea of uncertainly scares you to the core.

This thinking trap aligns with another: *Labeling*.

This is when we take one isolated incident and assign it to ourselves as a character trait. A mom made one mistake, but fell into the half-truth thinking trap of labeling herself a "Bad Mom." Perhaps you order greasy takeout for dinner instead of making something, and label yourself "Unhealthy." We take something that actually occurred in some sense (truth), then twist it to believe a lie about ourselves.

When you find yourself engaging in Catastrophizing, All-or-Nothing, or Labeling thinking traps, I'd prompt you to ask yourself, "Would I give my friend the same advice?"

I typically challenge this thought by thinking of it as a role-reversal exercise. If I saw my friend without her makeup, would I judge her? What if I stopped over and there was a sink full of dishes—would I care?

We are often times way harder on ourselves than we ever would imagine being to a friend. Let's be kind to ourselves!

Others find their feet caught in another thinking trap called *Overgeneralizing*. Essen-tially, Overgeneralizing is painting with a broad brush, implying that because one thing happened, something else (or everything else) will also happen (and/or will always hap-pen). The half-truth gets lumped into a guarantee that whatever scenario occurred is permanent and life-altering. We take an isolated event and use it to determine that things will always or never be the same again.

When we engage in this thinking trap, we are not using reasoning. We're using our emotions. Overgeneralizing is closely tied with the thinking trap of *Emotional Reasoning*, which is when we believe our feelings are facts.

For us moms, I recommend that we first "own" why we are Overgeneralizing. This is key in situations where you are making joint decisions with your husband about your child's future. If you are like me, you may feel the need to prove your point of view in order to gain your way in the situation you are overgeneralizing. I have found that it is much better just to own it. It can go something like this:

"I understand that it's irrational to think (the issue) and that I'm Overgeneralizing. I am not ready to (the objection) and I'm working on it; but for now,
I'm not ready."

I have found that my husband is always way more willing to act out of my Overgeneralization and Emotional Reasoning when I own it rather than when I argue it. So
next time *that thing* causes you to feel anxious—whether it's sleepovers, public school,
that new friend your child made—own it first and dedicate to work on it over time
intentionally.

The last thinking trap we'll cover happens when we are having a conversation with
someone and start filling in the blanks with everything we believe they must be thinking. Inserting things that are not supported by facts, things that were not actually said,
and yet acting as if they are true are a recipe for *Assuming*.

I know that when I do this, I then begin to act toward that person with the same attitude as if they actually said those things. Sometimes the best way to tackle this head-on is
by being blunt. Go ahead! I give you permission to ask. It can sound something like this:

"I'm sorry, I feel as if my story is boring you. Did I catch you at a bad time?"

"I apologize if I overstepped by asking that question. Did I offend you?"

"Oh, there I go again…did I say something that offended you?"

For me personally, I began doing this a lot after I became mom. I would feed my son
a bottle and mind-read: "I bet they are judging me right now for not breastfeeding." Or
I would share that my son attends public school, and I'd instantly mind-read, thinking,
"I bet they think I'm choosing my career over my kids." I am here to say nobody has said
either of those things to me, yet I have *assumed* it plenty of times. Gaining the courage
to address it will be difficult, but it will bring freedom.

ANXIETY IS AVOIDANCE

Anxiety often triggers the desire within us to escape. It tells us to avoid. Run! It tells
us *that thing* on our mind is extremely dangerous and we must flee like our life depends
on it. We must avoid it at all costs.

Anxiety festers and grows when we avoid it. It wants you to shape your actions to comply. It does this by making a circumstance bigger than what it should be. It puffs it up in our minds to take over our thoughts completely.

As moms, we avoid when placed in situations more times than we'd like to admit or even really know. Our mom anxiety, and thus avoidance, makes an appearance through overprotection. This is generally when we limit activities and opportunities for our children for our benefit rather than the benefit of the child. Basically, *we* are uncomfortable, so even when *they* are not, the answer is still always "No." We justify why they shouldn't participate, but if we are really honest, we are avoiding the situation due to our own anxiety. It's an "us" thing.

We might avoid play dates, social functions, schooling options, family gatherings, conversations about certain topics, vacations, or church not because we have a true conviction on why our child shouldn't participate but because it makes *us* anxious.

Physiologically, we are training our brain each time that avoiding was the correct response. When we are feeling anxious about something, generally we are thinking of the worst-possible scenario. When you focus and meditate on the worst-possible scenario, your brain believes you. Your brain begins to believe this is a real threat.

The facts say that the worst-case scenario only has a 0.001% probability of occurring. Perseverating on it inflates the statistics until our brains believe we're facing a fifty-fifty chance of that terrible situation. When we listen to our brain's misinformed instructions and avoid, our body feels relief as if to say, "Thank you! You just diverted that crisis. Well done!" But was there a real crisis? Absolutely not. We were making a mountain out of a worm hole. What actually happened was we robbed ourselves and our child of a potential growing experience due to that anxious thinking. Anxiety came knocking at the door and came out victorious.

Allowing anxiety to call the shots programs dangerous code into the brain.

Next time we are placed in an uncomfortable situation that makes us anxious, our brains will go in overdrive to avoid again. I mean, we can't blame it. We told our brains that it worked. So, that avoidance strategy will become more and more demanding, leading to isolation and even depression.

I know that's a lot of tough information to take in at once, but identifying the thinking traps is a big part of stopping them. And that's what fighting anxiety is: putting a stop to the unhealthy thought patterns.

ANXIETY IS A SPIRITUAL BATTLE

"Humble yourselves, therefore, under the mighty hand of God so that at the proper time he may exalt you, casting all your anxieties on him, because he cares for you. Be sober-minded; be watchful. Your adversary the devil prowls around like a roaring lion, seeking someone to devour. Resist him, firm in your faith."

1 Peter 5:6-9

Let's practice some righteous anger here and tell the lion to get out of our field! The lion will make its home here no longer. Simply telling the thought to leave will not make it flee. We need to challenge the lion to a duel. Just as with any other kind of war, peace is the result of a battle.

This war involves us challenging the illogical portion of the thought. My guess is that the thought has *some* level of truth. That is what makes the father of lies so cunning. He will not use a bold-face lie; he will be crafty. He will use a half-truth, which is ultimately a lie.

To challenge his lies and poke the flaws in the half-truth, I want you to ask some questions. Just as if the thought was on trial and you are about to cross-examine it. You will ask questions that reveal and prove the lie. Some of the questions I recommend include:

> What is the actual probability of this occurring?
> Has God talked about this in His Word? If so, what does he say?
> Would I give my friend the same advice if the roles were reversed?
> If the worse-case scenario actually does occur, will I be able to cope?

Handing over your anxiety onto God is the next step of healing. Going to war is a traumatic experience. Even if you won the war, you may still come out with wounds. These wounds need treatment in order to heal properly. That treatment involves talking about what happened, what was and is hard, and what you want to change first with God and then with trusted allies.

While handing over the burden of anxious thoughts to God is the first step, doing this in isolation will not fully heal the wound. We need to stich it up to ensure it doesn't become infected. We need to ensure it heals and doesn't open back up. The lion's favorite place to attack is an existing wound. You're more sensitive to pain there, your stitches

Simply telling the thought to leave will not make it flee. We need to challenge the lion to a duel. Just as with any other kind of war, peace is the result of a battle.

still mending, and that makes those places vulnerable. Why attack the healthiest part of the body? He goes for what is weak.

In order for the wound to be closed, you need to replace the thought. If you find yourself going to war again and again over the same issue, chances are you are winning, but you are not closing the wound. You are leaving yourself vulnerable to the lion because you are still engaging in the same thoughts. You are not rewriting your story.

Replacing the thought can be thought of like a vaccine (which is when we allow a non-harmful strain of a sickness into our body so our body learns to recognize it and build an immune system against it). It's a remedy that will lessen the attack. The threat is still there, but you will have a level of protection once you begin thinking differently. Replacing the thought is the difference between a defeated mom who is continually in the battlefield, and a mom who rests in her victory. It goes a little something like this:

> "I will no longer believe *(fill in that anxious thought),* and when that thought
> comes knocking, I'll remember and repeat *(this)* instead."

I encourage journaling for this part. When I work with anxious mamas, they journal about the war. I mean, everyone loves a good war story. They have all the juicy details and the raw emotion that make for a good story. She reads back and believes that's the end of the story. The reality is, when that trigger or circumstance presents itself again, she'll end up in the battlefield again. It was not the end. It was the plot.

The conclusion needs to be a surprise ending. The thought she will now think and believe going forward. It's absolutely beneficial to journal about the war for processing purposes. For therapeutic purposes, the focus should be on the change you intend to implement in specifics. When the problematic thinking traps come back, you will have a resource to review.

ANXIETY IS SILENT

I wonder how many of you are struggling in silence right now. You've identified with the symptoms of anxiety and you feel captive. You don't ever talk about it.

There was a study done this past year (2022) that asked women why they didn't seek help for their anxious thoughts and feelings. The results yielded many statistics, but the one that really stood out to me was twenty-five percent said they didn't know where to start.

Let me go first.

In addition to driving over bridges, I have a very intense fear of staying home alone at night. It's really quite intense the anxiousness that comes over me. I engage in the thinking trap of Catastrophizing. One creak and I can convince myself someone is in my house. I believe there really is someone that is going to come hurt me and my children. In addition to Catastrophizing, I also struggle with Overgeneralization. My body responds to all my fearful emotions, and I do something to calm my body down instead of challenging the half-truth.

I really wish I could avoid it at times, but I can't. Do you want to hear the real kicker? My husband travels for a living! Ha, yep. There is no way around this. It's something I'm working on overcoming.

I didn't start making progress though until I owned it. I confided in a few close friends. I asked for help. I talked with someone. I identified the thinking traps at play. I owned that it's silly and mostly irrational, yet accepted that it's very real to me. We live in a safe neighborhood and we have the security alarm set. I am safe. But all the firewalls and security systems in the world probably wouldn't settle the fear because it could never be soothed by facts. It was never *rooted* in facts.

My motivation to fight it was really motivated by my children. One day, they saw me looking out the window and started getting spooked themselves. My son asked me if there was someone out there, and I'll never forget the look of concern on his face. I was ashamed. I was mad at myself. How could I let my anxiety affect him like that? That was too far.

We were safe. Yet, I allowed my fear to overtake me. It was then I decided this was worth the work. It began by talking, though.

If you are of the twenty-five percent of moms who say they don't know where to begin, start with a good friend. Just the sentence, "I've been having a lot of anxious thoughts lately." Share with them what you feel comfortable sharing, and lean on their support as they ask how they can help you. Sometimes that is all we need. Don't feel like a failure though if that isn't enough support and you need to meet with a reputable therapist. It's not something that goes away without work, and our kids are worth that work. They watch how we treat ourselves, and it's not a matter of *if* we will pass down our anxiety but to *what degree* they will internalize our fears, thinking traps, and coping mechanisms.

THE END OF THE STORY

Whether you are *Mom A* who says you know you have anxiety, *Mom B* who says she thinks she may, or *Mom C* who says she's mostly free—we are all tempted. The degree to which we fight anxiety varies in frequency and intensity, but the temptation is there for us all. It will inevitably make an appearance on the road of motherhood.

I wish I could guarantee your *worst fear* will never come true. But like everything, God is bigger than our worst fears. There's hope even when the circumstances do not go our way. You can have peace and joy despite your circumstances. How that's possible doesn't have to make sense—God's peace surpasses all understanding (Philippians 4:6).

CHAPTER ELEVEN

Look Up

Look Up

had never been more exhausted in my life. We had just arrived home with our beautiful boy all the way from China, but we had to travel twenty-eight straight hours. With the time change, we had experienced no night. We drove from inland China to Hong Kong to depart, needing to switch cars twice. We transferred flights. We arrived in Chicago during a snowstorm. We navigated the blowing snow over an hour to our house.

It didn't matter. We were home. Home *sweet* home.

I remember dreaming of the day I could show Drake, who was almost two years old, his room. It was so welcoming and filled with toys. I was so tired though. It was honestly such a blur. Thankfully, I took a video of us walking up the stairs to show him because I don't otherwise remember it. Seeing the footage, I recall how the room was spinning from fatigue. We both needed to sleep, but we had a child now—who was very much awake. How was this going to work? We figured the room was baby-proofed, right? So we closed the door, collapsed flat on our faces on his bedroom floor, and fell asleep.

I was slightly jarred from my deep sleep at some point because I swear the doorbell rang. I saw Drake playing with his new toys beside me though, so I fell right back to sleep. I didn't care who was at the door. It didn't matter. You couldn't pay me to get off that floor. I was *that* tired! There were so many people praying and awaiting our arrival. I figured someone couldn't wait any longer and wanted to meet Drake. I could wait though. There was nothing in me that was ready to visit. The doorbell rang several more times, but each time, I fell back asleep.

The person then began knocking on the door. Relentlessly. Finally I could not ignore it anymore. When I walked downstairs and opened the door, I saw my neighbor. She was there to inform me we had left the car running with the hatch open for the past three hours in the snow! Thank goodness for neighbors.

STRENGTH BUILDING FROM GOD

Exhaustion stories are funny—and I want to hear yours one day. But they're also a clear demonstration how we can burn out in any form of rest deprivation, not just sleep.

Even on the day-to-day, without traveling around the globe, we can feel on-the-floor, car-running-outside tired. Our brain is an internet browser and for every tab we close, the world opens five new ones. We need to buy the stuff for school. We need to clean the house, pack the lunch, all while remembering to feed the animals and refill that prescription. We really do need some divine horsepower to carry ourselves through the terrain. Once again, the Bible reminds us how God gives us this strength:

> *"See, the Sovereign Lord comes with power,*
> *and he rules with a mighty arm.*
> *He tends his flock like a shepherd:*
> *He gathers the lambs in his arms*
> *and carries them close to his heart;*
> *he gently leads those that have young."*
>
> Isaiah 40:10-11

Hopefully this passage makes your ears perk up a bit. We lead young, and Isaiah tells us God wants to lead all the people who do just that—parents. Just as we lead our children, He wants to lead us. He knows we need His strength.

In the time this is thought to have been written, the Israelites were held captive by Babylon. At one time, God's people were freed, but once again they fell at the hands of a violent empire. They had reached a low point as God's people; still, God showed up to comfort and strengthen them in the midst of it through the prophecies of Isaiah.

History shows us that they were displaced from their homes and held captive. It is hard for me to grasp their reality, uprooted from their homes, communities, and way of life with little ones to protect and lead too. I am so grateful that God meets our need for strength, even mentioning specifically *those who have young*. As the Father of each Israelite child walking in turmoil then, He was being a strong parent. Today, He is still providing us with the wisdom and power we need to traverse all the ways our worlds become uprooted.

God meets the big needs, but He also meets the small everyday needs. Whether it be a sick child, a rebellious teenager, or just an exhausted mama after a long journey, we can all relate with needing strength from the same source: our great Shepherd.

Isaiah shares that God gathers us in His arms and leads us. He's tender and intimate, holding us to His sides—yet He also has a mighty hand, empowering us beyond what we needed. One way He gives us His strength is by changing our perspective. Our bodies are capable of so much more than we give them credit for. I'm sure you've heard of emergency situations where people developed an adrenaline rush of strength when placed in a life-or-death situation. Simply watch one of those "World's Strongest Men" competitions where they pull giant equipment, or Ninja Warrior shows where they monkey themselves through intense obstacles. God made our bodies to endure a lot with the strength He provides.

I've recently been introduced to the amount of physical strength it takes to be a mother as baby Zachary grows to be a chunkster. He is a big boy for one, and his car seat is massively heavy. I have never considered myself a strong lady. Yet, after this season of life, I have some renewed confidence. I can hold him for hours, lift the car seat above my chest to wiggle between the cars, and lift the stroller multiple times a day in and out of the trunk—all while wearing the baby backpack filled with everything under the sun. Being a mom requires some pretty hefty physical strength.

Even though we develop "baby gun" biceps and can carry our weight in laundry, sometimes God gives us a change of perspective to renew our internal strength. We don't always need more physical muscle but mental stamina to stay alert, involved, and positive with our life. We may be feeling weary, but if God can provide us hope, that will motivate us to continue despite being exhausted.

HELPING HANDS FROM GOD

We can also have our strength renewed with an actual physical answer to prayer. God may very well provide the strength that we lack.

I love the passage in Exodus, the first time God freed His people from captivity, when Moses was literally given a helping hand. Moses had just brought God's people through the Red Sea on dry ground. You remember that story, right? Moses went to Pharaoh repeatedly and said, "Let my people go." God then freed His people after sending the ten plagues and splitting the sea for them to pass.

> *Whenever Moses held up his hand, Israel prevailed, and whenever he*
> *lowered his hand, Amalek prevailed. But Moses' hands grew weary, so*
> *they took a stone and put it under him, and he sat on it, while Aaron*
> *and Hur held up his hands, one on one side, and the other on the other*
> *side. So, his hands were steady until the going down of the sun.*
>
> Exodus 17:11-12

God was with His people and provided physical strength to have them prevail. "Amalek," or the Amalekites, were a people in the Bible that the Israelites fought with more than once. When they are mentioned here, Moses used the tools and strength God instructed of him to protect and strengthen their men. In this story, Moses' hands literally demonstrate how God had His hands over their people, and how the elders Aaron and Hur supported Moses. It's one of those passages in the Bible that's both amazing and really strange if you don't believe in God. If we closed on Exodus 17, the Israelites had a nice, "happily ever after." The story does not end with the defeat of the Amalekites, though. If you read on, God's people continually face hardships (mostly self-induced, but hey, I think I can relate). God never gives up on them, though. In this very scenario they were fighting a war and despite their shortcomings and weaknesses (and even self-induced troubles), God still came to their aid.

There is no doubt that if you call on the Father, He will show up for you too! Even when He's at the "gym" with me every day, doing strength training workouts, I can actually forget (or become "nose-blind" if you remember that term) that He's the one providing for me.

I tend to pay less attention to the one-on-one internal training and more on the obvious, like finding a babysitter, special events at the library, or everyone dodging the stomach flu my husband brought home. God's provision of strength to us—the giddy-up in our physical, mental, spiritual, and emotional stamina every day—is delivered differently and on a spectrum of subtlety. But all of these perfectly timed blessings are given to us for exactly the right reason and to deliver us through our situation.

God's provision of strength to us—the giddy-up in our physical, mental, spiritual, and emotional stamina every day—is delivered differently and on a spectrum of subtlety.

REST IS HOLY

The last way I see God giving us strength is through the Sabbath. This was intended to be a built-in rest day for creation—one where we can renew our bodies so they can be equipped to do the great. Resting was God's intent when everything in the world was perfect. He created the Sabbath before the fall of man, meaning that rest is a holy practice—not just a physical requirement. After sin and evil entered the world, the concept of resting became even more necessary and for much more varied reasons, but God introduced the Sabbath to connect us as a way to give us strength.

Adrenaline is typically accessed during extenuating circumstances that trigger an alarm in our brain and hormones. For regular life, our bodies require a steady and sustainable pace that fits our daily lifestyle. Additionally, the helping hand God gives us in our moments of exhaustion, defeat, or battle are not typically consistent occurrences, nor are they intended to be. The emotional strength God gives us, as described in Isaiah, comes to us in many ways (like prayer), but also in the dedicated time we create for God on our Sabbath. Even God Himself rested on the Sabbath not because He needed anything from anyone but because it was holy and important to Him. Our all-powerful, omnipotent, omnipresent Lord chose to rest:

> *"Thus, the heavens and the earth were finished, and all the host of*
> *them. And on the seventh day God finished his work that he had*
> *done, and he rested on the seventh day from all his work that he had*
> *done. So God blessed the seventh day and made it holy, because on*
> *its God rested from all his work that he had done in creation."*
>
> **Genesis 2:1-3**

We are foolish to believe we are exempt from this discipline. That we can skip out and still make it through our week. Engaging in the Sabbath is doing what is needed. It's not a "bonus" for good behavior. It's not meant to be a luxury. It's not something that we should earn if we *were really productive this week*. Resting truly is a need and a requirement. It's something that God commands and uses to equip us to continue the hard work of motherhood.

God doesn't say we *deserve* it. God says we *require* it, like food and water.

That is what makes rest even more beautiful. It is a gift given to us by the Lord. So, when you are feeling weary physically, and your exhaustion leads to feeling tattered, be assured that God answers prayers for strength. He provides change of perspective, physical help, and a Sabbath day of rest.

Rest looks different for everyone today. Sleeping, hiking, getting a massage, running, writing, or maybe sewing. A whole day, a half day, or just two sacred hours.

Our pace and attitude about it affect our kids. On the other six days of the week, our lifestyle is intended to be joyful and attentive. That's a tall order in the modern world, though. The technological advancements I see advertised are often centered on maximizing productivity. Our culture likes to multitask.

If we have to do laundry, at least put on a show, right? In the lulls of elevator rides, waiting rooms, and meetings about to start, our phones suddenly have compelling things to show us. And on the days when nothing in the kitchen inspires us to cook or clean, or you have back-to-back commitments, dinner gets eaten while driving.

Doing two things at once is not inherently wrong—if it's working for you, awesome! Everything in moderation. God's ability to strengthen us is through rest, though. Cramming everything together in our days to eliminate "wasted time" between each activity is the name of the game if we're not careful. I've noticed that sometimes since having kids, I use the excuse "Mama needs a rest" for moments that aren't actually refreshing or energizing me. And my boys notice. Kids pay attention to how we use the word "rest," among other things.

When we never stop, never look up and around us, we subtly teach them that this form of rest is not valued or even exists! God is present in our daily lives, not just when we pray before dinner and bedtime or read a devotional. But He needs us to put down the busy-work or screens that tune Him out. Our children are watching us, and they will model what they see.

A behaviorist by the name of Albert Bandura noticed we can learn things from other people's experiences. He was interested in how exposure alone could shape the way we go on to behave. His hypothesis was tested many times, deemed valid by peers as a proven theory, and it became known as the "social learning theory." He determined that children do learn by watching and copying others.[21]

Bandura ran the famous "Bobo Doll" experiment, where he had an adult act aggressively toward a toy in front of their child. The toy was then provided to their child at a later date, and what do you think the child did with the toy? Yep—the exact same thing they observed the adult do. They treated the toy with hostility. Bandura went on to advocate that parents should pay attention to what they expose their children to because the way they act shapes the way their kids may behave.

If we really believe that rest is important, then *we* are going to have to *rest*. Our children are watching, and I'm sure they will gladly cuddle up with you on the couch!

EYES ON HIM, MAMAS

It is so easy, ladies, to look to our left and our right and see the women that have visible strength. We assess another mom's ability and measure it up against our own. With all sorts of metrics, the bottom line is whatever other moms are able to deadlift, we need to be able to lift too.

How does she make it to all her son's track meets, make organic meals, have so many friends, wear such cute and formal clothes all day, all while homeschooling five children? We see all that she *does* and think that equates her strength. We envy that strength. We try to find their secret recipe to be the energizer bunny, constantly being pulled in every direction and yet doing so with such ease.

This is where God steps in and commands our hearts to focus on the long game. When we begin to compare, we're putting our Moses Hand down—letting the opposing side win. God strengthens those who have their eyes on Him, not on the ones they envy. His strength will probably not replicate what our eyes see in those we envy.

The only way for us to gain the strength we need is to seek the Lord and His timing. We may think *that Mom* has the secret, but the answer lies with God alone. Read His Word, pray, recognizing out loud or internally that we need Him before the day even begins—then again throughout our days and probably after the days end. Waiting on God is having a thankful attitude about how He has given us strength yesterday and trusting that He will do it again today.

HANGRY AND OVERTIRED

A prophet named Elijah in the Old Testament loved the Lord deeply and was audacious in his servanthood. He did some pretty amazing things by healing people and casting down false gods in the name of the one true God. In 1 Kings 18, he initiated a great challenge against King Ahab and their false god, Baal. Elijah called on God to light a fire to prove he was true. King Ahab was to ask the same of Baal. God showed up in a mighty way, igniting the fire and proving His power. When King Ahab asked his god to light a fire, no such fire appeared (as you can probably imagine).

When we begin to compare, we're putting our

Moses Hand down—letting the opposing side win.

God strengthens those who have their eyes on Him,

not on the ones they envy.

Elijah should have been celebrating. We might have assumed he rode that spiritual "high" for a while. That was a great victory! Unfortunately, Elijah began to crumble after that moment. The men of King Ahab now wanted him dead due to the humiliation he caused them, and Elijah had to escape. He ran deep into the woods, fell under a tree, and began to wish for death (1 Kings 19:4). He was depleted and afraid.

Okay, it's a little hard to sympathize for Elijah in this moment. He *just saw* the power of God at work! Why was he so afraid of the people now? God clearly showed up when he challenged them the day before. He would definitely be safe from anything else.

What happens next is as significant as it is silly:

> *"And he lay down and slept under a broom tree. And behold, an angel touched*
> *him and said to him, 'Arise and eat.' And he looked, and behold, there*
> *was at his head a cake baked on hot stones and a jar of water. And he ate*
> *and drank and lay down again. And the angel of the* Lord *came again a*
> *second time and touched him and said, 'Arise and eat, for the journey is too*
> *great for you.' And he arose and ate and drank, and went in the strength*
> *of that food forty days and forty nights to Horeb, the mount of God."*
>
> 1 Kings 19:5-8

In the most literal way, this story has made more than a few readers chuckle. Elijah just sounded like a dramatic case of hanger (or whatever you call being hungry-sad)! The moody, woe-is-me whining we're all guilty of today when we go too long without eating and staying hydrated. But of course, Elijah was braving much heavier struggles than that comedic take.

Elijah was physically exhausted from running and likely even the stress of his life before the king called for his head. The same way we get melodramatically irritable when our stomachs need food, bodies that haven't had a chance to rest or sleep for too long also devolve into poor emotional regulation and perception. Just ask toddlers who skip their naps. So even though Elijah *saw* his Father light the altar on fire, and even though Elijah got to communicate *directly* with God, he still lost hope. All the proof in the world would not register in his brain in the best way until his physical needs were met, but he couldn't recognize that in his weariness. He was spiritually vulnerable. He was afraid. He wanted to die.

In my perspective, our heavenly Father embodied the empathetic encourager in that moment. Maybe he saw Elijah's feelings and held back a giggle the way some of our own kids' tantrums make us laugh. Maybe a human father would grow frustrated by Elijah's plea under the tree, angry that he could be so ungrateful. But God loves His children perfectly. He sent an angel to comfort this important child of His with food and water, like taking care of us when we're sick and need to take medicine. God heard Elijah, He felt compassion for him, and He strengthened him with what he needed in the perfect time, place, and pace to complete his duties.

How beautiful a story that God would send his angels to feed us. How heartwarming to know that we have a God who serves over lectures. We sometimes need a lecture, but God knew what Elijah needed first was nutrition and rest, and that is exactly what He provided.

Beyond just eating and sleeping before the tears and fights break loose, this story illustrated true rest.

OUR KIDS ROCK!

I was at the park once where a boy was stacking rocks. He kept trying to make the pile higher, but when he'd add the top rock, the stack would always fall over. After the third tumble, he was starting to get frustrated. He looked up at his mom, and she simply responded with an encouraging head nod followed by a smile. It was all he needed.

He bent over and began picking up the rocks again, attempting to make the pile higher. When he finally got it up, he went over to his mom, who praised him so loudly the whole park could hear.

Why are moms so invested in these moments? To some, these moments seem too insignificant for such an incredulous celebration. It's because our *children* are significant. They are the most valuable people in our lives. We love them so deeply that when we can do anything to help them along, regardless of how "valuable" the task, we show up.

This exactly who God is too. He is our Father, and we are His children. When planning out the week, we may have written things like which days to have bath time, meal prep, library book due dates, and can't-put-it-off-anymore chores like mopping the floor down. Perhaps these tasks within themselves are insignificant on paper. God sees them through our eyes, though. And mamas, because we are so important and meaningful to our Father, He genuinely does throw confetti for us when we return library books on time.

He's not waiting to show up for the grand finale, only when we *do it right*, or only when we cry out for a lifeline loud enough. He shows up wherever we are, every time, with a perfect punch card. Every time we turn off our alarm and slow-foot to the kitchen, He's already there with His Word and a coffee for me. That's the first strength I need in the morning every time.

CHAPTER TWELVE

Learning As We Grow

Abeautiful and holy part of motherhood is the desire to improve. We are convicted. There are things that grab at our heart and tell us to try harder, pray more, and lean in. This, mama, is good. *This is very good.*

It's good because it means you have a relationship with the heavenly Father. The God who wants to shape us to be more like Him. The God who wants to use us in great ways. God who is love. God who will work His love through you to be the best mama you can be. If you didn't have a relationship with God, you wouldn't recognize and care about the great work He's doing in your life. While it's good, really acting on what you have learned and are learning often takes us out of our comfort zones. We're not easily convinced to leave our comfort zones unless we really trust our leader.

Excellence in motherhood isn't just something that God wants for us. We joyfully join Him. We know it will be hard, but we are all in. We have recognized our need for growth, seen areas that are lacking, and care enough to do something about it. We're not just saying, "I should really do something about that." You've dedicated your time through this text to work at it. You've processed, reflected, and made some tangible goals.

As you keep moving and growing, keep your eyes on the Father, not on the goals. Without remembering why we strive for excellence, we are easy targets for Mom Guilt. Some are prone to walk around with it like a badge of honor. They meditate day and night on their shortcomings. They wonder what life would be like if they were better. They focus on the negative, and begin to believe that they are as worthless as their imagination tells them. That's built on a half-truth, and that is *Mom Guilt.*

If you are not on guard, the exciting leap toward getting to know our kids and love

Excellence in motherhood isn't

just something that God wants

for us. We joyfully join Him.

We know it will be hard, but

we are all in.

them better can evolve into work-based motherhood. Focusing on the external. The checklist of good deeds, things society told us we need to get done, and lifestyle qualities our circles swear changes everything. I love checklists as much as the next mom, but those are just tools to help us stay organized. They are not the prize, receipt, or timesheet that proves we got our hours in.

Parenting books offer a lot of unique premises. Many moms read parenting books for encouragement. It gets hard and they need a good pick-me-up. Others are reaching for them to gain an education. They want to be schooled in motherhood, to grow and develop even more. Some want funny stories, others want specific guidance, while a few are reading things for a book club, Bible study, or within a friend circle. Sadly, some are grasping for them out of desperation. They have a particular area of concern, and they are desperately searching for the black-and-white solution to their problem, conflict, or need.

I get sad thinking of the mom who reads parenting books to rid her of the guilt she continually feels. She might continue to gain head knowledge but only see a gap growing between where they are and where they are told they need to be.

I have desperately wished that by learning more, I could close that gap between what I want to be (or think I should be) and where I am. I still struggle some days with that guilt and shame. When we come to the end of a motherhood book like this, the gap seems really far.

But we all have a choice to make. We can rest in God's plan and grace in our lives, or we can wallow in the Mom Guilt and hope that carries us over. The gap will always be there.

God is the perfect bridge for us. We are given permission to embrace motherhood because we know we have all that our kids require to walk with Him too.

PRAYERS

My prayer is that you will not give up the desire to be your best in order to selfishly avoid seeing where you fall short.

My prayer is that you will continually learn and open yourself to God's Word and rich guidance despite the reality that you'll never meet it all. It's okay, though. You do not have to be perfect today or on earth. Everything is made perfect in its time.

My prayer is that we will not think of ourselves too highly than we ought, and that we will continually see the need to develop, mature, and grow. We will never think that we have arrived and stop picturing ourselves as God's kid, still growing up.

My prayer is that we do not give up or slow down reading God's Word. I pray we will never think we are "spiritual enough" or "close enough" to God that we can forfeit the beauty of what He offers us daily. If we climb the tree of self-righteousness, it may be a long fall before we reach God at the bottom who will still consistently catch us.

My prayer is that we can walk the gray line of self-improvement and sanctification without self-deprivation. This is a tall task, but truly the secret to continually improve in motherhood. Continue with confidence, not guilt or shame. We know we'll fall, but we trust that God's walking with us.

I pray we notice that every time we do fall, the distance is a little bit shorter in some ways. Our legs grew longer, our feet sturdier, or our arms stronger on those monkey bars because the last time we fell, we learned, we moved forward, and we grew.

I pray God will cut back the weeds that feel suffocating and provide us each with perfect peach tree soil to support the process of new life. He's reliable and consistently there for us, pouring living water into our thirsty roots.

I pray that with time, you can repeat and affirm that even when you may not get it right all the time,

you are learning as you grow.

References

CHAPTER 1

1. Barna, George. 2010. Revolutionary Parenting: What the Research Shows Really Works. Carol Stream, Ill.: Tyndale House Publishers

CHAPTER 2

2. Fitzpatrick, Elyse, and Jessica Thompson. 2011. Give Them Grace: Dazzling Your Kids with the Love of Jesus. Wheaton, Ill.: Crossway.

CHAPTER 3

3. Gillihan, Seth. Cognitive Behavioral Therapy Made Simple : 10 Strategies for Managing Anxiety, Depression, Anger, Panic, and Worry. Emeryville, Ca: Althea Press, 2018.

4. Modecki, Kathryn L., Jeannie Minchin, Allen G. Harbaugh, Nancy G. Guerra, and Kevin C. Runions. "Bullying Prevalence across Contexts: A Meta-Analysis Measuring Cyber and Traditional Bullying." Journal of Adolescent Health 55, no. 5 (November 2014): 602–11. https://doi.org/10.1016/j.jadohealth.2014.06.007.

CHAPTER 4

5. Tolman, Edward C. 1948. "Cognitive Maps in Rats and Men." Psychological Review 55 (4): 189–208. https://doi.org/10.1037/h0061626.

6. Mandal, Manisha Deb, and Shyamapada Mandal. "Honey: Its Medicinal Property and Antibacterial Activity." Asian Pacific Journal of Tropical Biomedicine 1, no. 2 (April 2011): 154–60. https://doi.org/10.1016/s2221-1691(11)60016-6.

7. Maslow, Abraham. 1943. "Preface to Motivation Theory." Psychosomatic Medicine 5 (1): 85–92. https://doi.org/10.1097/00006842-194301000-00012.

8. Murdock, Bennet B. 1985. "The Contributions of Hermann Ebbinghaus." Journal of Experimental Psychology: Learning, Memory, and Cognition 11 (3): 469–71. https://doi.org/10.1037/0278-7393.11.3.469.

CHAPTER 5

9. Loftus, Elizabeth F. 1996. Eyewitness Testimony. Cambridge, Mass.: Harvard University Press.

10. Matthys, Walter, and Dennis J. L. G. Schutter. "Improving Our Understanding of Impaired Social Problem-Solving in Children and Adolescents with Conduct Problems: Implications for Cognitive Behavioral Therapy." Clinical Child and Family Psychology Review, no. 25 (February 14, 2022). https://doi.org/10.1007/s10567-021-00376-y.

CHAPTER 6

11. Miner, John B. 2005. Organizational Behavior. Vol. 1. Armonk, N.Y.: M.E. Sharpe.

12. Berle, David, Michelle L. Moulds, Vladan Starcevic, Denise Milicevic, Anthony Hannan, Erin Dale, Kirupamani Viswasam, and Vlasios Brakoulias. "Does Emotional Reasoning Change during Cognitive Behavioural Therapy for Anxiety?" Cognitive Behaviour Therapy 45, no. 2 (January 6, 2016): 123–35. https://doi.org/10.1080/16506073.2015.1115892.

13. Carter, Marc. 2012. "Review of Thinking, Fast and Slow by Daniel Kahneman." Inquiry: Critical Thinking across the Disciplines 27 (2): 50–53. https://doi.org/10.5840/inquiryct201227212.

14. Milgram, Stanley, and Alan Elms. 1966. "Personality Characteristics Associated with Obedience and Defiance toward Authoritative Command." Journal of Experimental Research in Personality 1 (4).

CHAPTER 7

15. Schlichenmeyer, Kevin J., William V. Dube, and Mariela Vargas-Irwin. 2015. "Stimulus Fading and Response Elaboration in Differential Reinforcement for Alternative Behavior." Behavioral Interventions 30 (1): 51–64. https://doi.org/10.1002/bin.1402.

16. Plavnick, Joshua B., and Matthew P. Normand. 2013. "FUNCTIONAL ANALYSIS of VERBAL BEHAVIOR: A BRIEF REVIEW." Journal of Applied Behavior Analysis 46 (1): 349–53. https://doi.org/10.1002/jaba.1.

CHAPTER 8

17. Shin, Eun Kyong, Kaja LeWinn, Nicole Bush, Frances A. Tylavsky, Robert Lowell Davis, and Arash Shaban-Nejad. "Association of Maternal Social Relationships with Cognitive Development in Early Childhood." JAMA Network Open 2, no. 1 (January 11, 2019): e186963. https://doi.org/10.1001/jamanetworkopen.2018.6963.

CHAPTER 9

18. Broadbent, Donald. 1958. "Perception and Communication." Pergamon Press.

19. Zajonc, R.B. 2001. "Mere Exposure: A Gateway to the Subliminal." Current Directions in Psychological Science 10 (6): 224–28. https://doi.org/10.1111/1467-8721.00154.

CHAPTER 10

20. Seth Gillihan, Cognitive Behavioral Therapy Made.

CHAPTER 11

21. Bandura, Albert, Dorothea Ross, and Sheila A. Ross. 1961. "Transmission of Aggression through Imitation of Aggressive Models." The Journal of Abnormal and Social Psychology 63 (3): 575–82. https://doi.org/10.1037/h0045925.

A Special Shout-Out

First and foremost, I thank my Lord and Savior Jesus Christ who loved me first. It's through His redemptive and undeserved love that I can do anything of significance.

Thank you to my loving and wise husband, John. Your behind-the-scenes sacrifices and support are truly what has made all this possible. While my name may be on the cover, any wisdom that I have to offer moms is just an overflow from your example and our late-night conversations on the couch after the boys fall asleep. While I do adore being "Mom," I love being your wife equally as much!

Thank you to my talented mother, Beth. I remember in kindergarten, there was a girl in my class who told me I was so lucky that you were *my* mom. It wasn't until I became a mom myself that I realized the deep truth behind those words. The creativity and fun you brought to my childhood reminds me never to forget joy while mothering. The artwork found in these pages are accredited to my own mother's talent, and I would be remiss if I didn't include them in my own teachings on motherhood.

Thank you to the fellow moms in my life who I love—my sisters (Jamie, Samantha, and Maigan), grandmother Rae, & mother-in-law Orthen.

Thank you to my Jackson Creek church family, Starlithawk Photography, Jenna Young Consulting followers, and friends so close they are family. So many of you prayed, encouraged, and supported this project from the very beginning—thank you!

Thank you to my editor, Abbey—who pushed me to do far more than I ever thought possible, and Jessica for being the first to read my work and encourage me to keep going.

Last but certainty not least, to you, my mom reader, thank you. It is a deep privilege that you would read and value my words. Children are blessings from God, and what a joy you are for me, a relatively new mom, in stewarding these amazing gifts. You were prayed over countless times as I wrote this for you. May we continuously strive to be the best moms we can be, side by side.

Jenna

About the Author

Jenna Young is both an adoptive and biological Mama who waited ten long years before God answered her prayer to be mom. She recognizes firsthand how special the gift of children is. She uses this passion alongside her calling as a behavior therapist to share helpful tools and raise awareness on how we can raise children using both God's Word and evidence-based practices.

Jenna is the founder of Jenna Young Consulting. If you would like to contact her, read more of her blog posts and content, welcome her to speak at your next event, or would be interested in individualized family services to bring about lasting change, you can find all of that and more at:

www.jennayoungconsulting.com

Made in the USA
Monee, IL
01 May 2023